THE STORYTELLER'S GODDESS

THE
STORYTELLER'S

GODDESS

Tales of the Goddess and Her Wisdom from Around the World

Carolyn McVickar Edwards

HarperSanFrancisco
A Division of HarperCollins*Publishers*

Illustrations by Kathleen Edwards

Verbal renderings of stories are encouraged as long as storyteller expressly credits this book.

THE STORYTELLER'S GODDESS: *Tales of the Goddess and Her Wisdom From Around the World*. Copyright © 1991 by Carolyn McVickar Edwards. Printed in the United States of America. No part of this book may be used or reproduced in any manner whatsoever without written permission except in the case of brief quotations embodied in critical articles and reviews. For information address HarperCollins Publishers, 10 East 53rd Street, New York, NY 10022.

FIRST EDITION

Library of Congress Cataloging-in-Publication Data
Edwards, Carolyn McVickar.
    The storyteller's goddess : tales of the goddess and her wisdom
from around the world / Carolyn McVickar Edwards. — 1st ed.
        p.   cm.
    Includes bibliographical references.
    ISBN 0–06–250263–8 (alk. paper)
    1. Goddesses.   I. Title.
BL473.5.E38   1991
291.2'114—dc20   90–56445
                                                                         CIP

91 92 93 94 95 RRD(H) 10 9 8 7 6 5 4 3 2 1

This edition is printed on acid-free paper that meets the American National Standards Institute Z39.48 Standard.

for Michael

Contents

III. Spirit Incarnate: Goddess As Earth and Body
75

IV. The Force of Life: Sexuality and Creativity
103

VII. Recovery of Herstory   191

Acknowledgments

I AM overflowing with gratitude at the idea that I am actually getting to write this page. I feel like thanking everyone I've ever met for affecting me, holding me, supporting me. Somehow I've made it to today: I'm alive and I'm well and I'm telling stories.

This book would never have happened without the incomparable work of Merlin Stone who wrote *Ancient Mirrors of Womanhood*, on which I have relied tremendously. I also owe a great deal of insight to Jean Shinoda Bolen's *Goddesses in Everywoman* and Barbara Walker's *The Woman's Encyclopedia of Myths and Secrets*. Many other authors responsible for inspiration for this work are listed in the Book List. Maureen Larkin lent me *Ancient Mirrors*, and Ellen Toomey told me about Ariadne Weaver's "Equal Rites for Women" class that was the occasion of my homecoming to Sacred Woman. Thanks to Donna Andrews; Danielle Berner; Jackie Braun; Z. Budapest; Susan Burke; Jean Calderaro; Frances Dean; Lenel D'Emma; Erin Donahue; Debbie Downer; Joanne Edel; Alan, Helen, Kathleen, Madeleine, and Norval Edwards; Meredith Ellen; Cynthia Evers; Sharon Frame; Rose Garfinkle; Johanna Gladieux; Leslie Grant; Carla Heins; Jean Jacote; Claire Jeanette; Sue Kubek; Gary Lebow; Genny LeMorgan; Marla Weber-Oliviera; Scott Parker; Renee Neville; Patrice Scott; Sandia Siegel; and Barbara Weigle. Thanks to my editor, Barbara Moulton, and her assistant, Barbara Archer. Thank you to Thomas Mills for his help with my writing over the five years I worked with him. Thanks to all the people with whom I have shared Twelve-Step meetings, and to the people who began those meetings in the 1930s. Thank you to all the people who have made circles and rituals with me.

Before I learned about the Goddess, I discovered the Moon. At twenty-eight, in another country, I suddenly, for the first time in my life, really *looked* at the moon. I have seen in Her ever since the face of a woman who alternately cries in pain and throws her head back in song. It is from my relationship to this stunning globe that I draw inspiration and strength. She is my mirror and my scope. She is now the Goddess for me, and in Her ever-changing simplicity I rest.

Introduction

STORIES are humankind's oldest way of talking about and taking in truths. In every society may be found stories that portray religious or cultural values to its people. From the Bhagavad Gita to the Bible, stories are the means by which people identify their deities and values and make them tangible.

Modern urban people, however, are becoming increasingly disconnected from gods and values that split mind from body, soul from Earth, and dark from wisdom. Some are inventing a new brand of culture, a new religion. Whether they are remembering it in states of creative trance, reconvening it from shards of history and anthropology, or winging it in candlelit living rooms, they are re-enchanting themselves with the Great Feminine Principle. By Her invocation, they are weaving a web of life with strands of death and the dark. They are telling their personal stories in the context of ritual: they are calling up ancient knowings mixed with right-now longing for healing, communal vulnerability, and everyday intimacy with Sister Earth. They call their religion Goddess spirituality, Earth-centered spirituality, Goddess consciousness, or neopaganism; all refer to the present-day revival of Earth-based religions and the sense that Earth is sacred and divine. It is an attitude and way of life practiced by many different ancient peoples and by groups of indigenous peoples today.

Like people from all times, we who long for the Goddess need Her stories to know Her. This book is a collection of thirty stories about thirty-four Goddesses from twenty cultures.* I have both found and invented these stories, spinning them from bits of herstory. Each story is accompanied by an introduction that places it in cultural and historical context, talks about the story's origin, and mentions the props I use to invoke that story's Goddess.

A treasury of Goddess stories cannot be complete. Her shapes and lore are too myriad for that. For me, this collection lacks at least the story of Nu Kua, the Great Snail Woman of ancient China; the story of Allat, Goddess of the Sun, who preceded the currently worshiped male God Allah of Islam; and a story that honors woman-for-woman sexual love on a divine scale.

One author's scope—of time and research—is bound to be limited. Other tellers, authors, parents, and teachers will talk and talk of the Goddess until Her lore permeates the culture. For Her face, in story form, is as many colored as our own. Her hands are as young and as weathered. Her truths are the paradoxical and sensual mysteries we seek. Her stories are meant to be shared aloud. Whether shouted into the wind at the edge of the sea, told in the candlelight of urban indoor ritual, or read at the edge of a child's bed, these stories are for the beginnings and deepenings of knowing Her without end.

---

*India, Ireland, Greece, and the Middle East are severally represented; Goddess worship in these cultures is current, close to the surface, or closely bound up with current secular or Judeo-Christian mythologies.

Seven Goddess Principles:
Truths Inside of Truths

IN WRITING this book, I mean to sit with you at the hearth of our mutual wonder and wisdom and to spin for you, Grandma style, stories and reflections about the Great Mother of us all. I hope that some of Her stories will become beloved to you— that all, snuggled in the context of seven principles that crystallize something of Her essence in my life, will crackle a certainty of Her inside you. Together we are reviving an ancient Earth-centered religion. We are sharing truths of Her that flow from each of us in order to make a whole as ever changing and powerful as the ocean.

The Goddess takes hundreds of forms; Her names and stories lie for us to piece together like shards of pottery in red earth. The stories in this book are the ones that came to me— largely from the inspiration of Merlin Stone's *Ancient Mirrors of Womanhood*—between 1984 and 1990. I have grouped them, according to seven Goddess principles, as follows:

I. **All in All: Healing the Split.**
The Goddess is both dark and light.
II. **Constant Change: The Everlasting Cycle.**
The Goddess is the endless circle of life and death.
III. **Spirit Incarnate: Goddess As Earth and Body.**
The Goddess is the stuff of the Planet and our fleshly selves.

IV. The Force of Life: Sexuality and Creativity.
The Goddess is everlasting, burgeoning desire.

V. Surrender.
The Goddess loosens cities from foundations and flesh from bones.

VI. Goddess As Archetype.
The Goddess is the Great Feminine of our individual and collective unconscious, emerging again for full and life-changing honor by our conscious selves.

VII. Recovery of Herstory.
The Goddess has been worshiped by civilizations of people whose reverence for Female and Earth has been smeared from history. In reclaiming that herstory, the story of ourselves as human becomes whole.

Once, when I was a little girl, I played for an afternoon with a set of Russian nesting dolls. I feel wistful even now thinking of them. They were sturdy and round, kindly, with rosy cheeks and painted smiles and shawls. They all looked exactly alike, except that none of them were the same size. Each got progressively smaller and came apart at her ample waist in order that all the smaller dolls fit inside. With immense satisfaction I played with their glossy little bodies, taking them apart (some of them, all of them), arranging them in patterns, returning them to their sisters' bellies, and counting them with all the dreamy keenness of a miser with her gold.

My seven Goddess principles feel like those Russian nesting dolls as I fondle their intricacies and imagine how they may fit together. The principles seem not hierarchical but concentric in relation to each other. The most flexible concept of the Goddess's totality of light and dark seems like the mama doll that holds within her all the other concepts. Like each doll, each principle can be examined separately, but each is fully itself when played with as part of a spiral of questions and truths.

Goddess principles invite wondering and questions along with their truths. This sense of continuous pondering and unfolding, like the surprise of the next doll in those sweet onion

4

layers, is perhaps most precious of all to me on this spiritual path. Continual discovery and truth-from-within counters the dogmatic forcefulness of the fundamentalist Christianity in which I was raised. In that religion, absolute truth lay in a book, and authorities frowned when I used my mind to question or object to the "facts" I was taught.

Goddess As Metaphor

Earth is Woman. This is the basic metaphor of Goddess-centered spirituality. Resacralizing Her, Earth and Woman, is now our task. Such a task it is! In it we stand, shadows and fiery projections of the women who will be and have been. Figures we are, like the Great Metaphoress Herself, with mountainous breasts and soft, valleyed bellies. Like rivers, the blood of Woman runs in us, encoding, preserving, and brandishing the rage, the tenderness, the sorrow, and the stories that change us.

How do we change? First, we take back, over and over again, the sacredness of our Woman selves: our bodies; our sexualities; our birth-giving, creation-making beings. Then we retrieve from misuse and abuse all the concepts the patriarchy relates to our femaleness: body, blood, under, deep, color, dark, below, wetness, depth, intuition, divination.

Next, when we open emotionally and spiritually to realizing Earth Herself as sacred Woman, we are stunned at the similarities between Her physical and psychological rapes and our own. Repeatedly, we find our new notions of individual selfhood curled like fetuses inside our understanding of our relationship to ourselves as Planet. When we think not as scientists but in service of our hearts, we find our personal recoveries paralleling the ecological recovery of the Planet.

Now, we begin to think of water as the blood of the Goddess, from Whose flow comes all life. We think of Earth as Her body and see Her curves in the hills and mountains; tree limbs begin to look like Her arms. We sense the air as Her breath, and the mystery of fire becomes Her will and Her spirit. In such an attitude of worship, we no longer take for granted electrical

5

lighting; nuclear poison is akin to the rape of a child by a father. When we call the weather the emotions of the Goddess, controlling and categorizing instead of respecting and honoring seem the efforts of a rigid, unimaginative parent. We call Earth Woman: Mother, Daughter, Sister, Baby, Crone, Child, Lover. We call Her Teacher, Doctor, Healer, Inventor. We look at the ways we are She and She is we, and we want to twirl in the subway station and shake out ribboned tambourines.

Is a metaphor real? To my way of understanding, metaphor is probably the most powerful and complete way to understand any significant concept. For me, the deepest spiritual concepts are elusive. My grasp on them comes and goes, depending on my current situation. And always they are ideas; I can't see them. I need to make my concepts tangible if I am to understand and grasp them on deeper than intellectual levels. When, for example, I envision the seasons of Earth as the Navajo people's Changing Woman, the inveterate turning of the world becomes as personal as my own menstrual cycle. In the Egyptian Goddess Isis, I know the cycle of the grains that keep me alive as I know a mother and her child. Knowing the Hebrew Shekina, I know wisdom as if She were a lover, ephemeral and thrillingly present at once.

Goddess spirituality is all about making spiritual truths tangible. More than that, spiritual truths in Goddess spirituality *are* tangible. In Earth-centered spirituality, the tangible, physical world is not shameful—something to dominate while we are here and to leave behind when we die. The physical in Goddess spirituality is the source of all that we are and know.

Where Does the Goddess Come From?

In cultures all over the world in all times, the image of the circle has been sacred. Before we had a spaceship to prove it, before maps were precise, humans sensed the circularity of life and the world. Humans have always known that the personal womb is life's entry point and the Earth's womb is its exit.

Before the present patriarchal times, humans expressed this knowledge in their conceptualization of the Creator as Mother.

They recognized their Creator as Preserver; they knew Her as Destroyer. They called Her hundreds of names: Danu, Kali, Mayahuel, Astarte. They divided Her into thousands of aspects in order to more precisely worship Her: Queen of Light, Ruler of the Underworld, Giver of Numbers and Strategy, Keeper of Pleasure, Lady of the Land. From our patriarchal perspective, we call Goddess-worshiping peoples indigenous, aboriginal, or rural. We observe that these people are invariably tied intimately to the land, and that they contact their environment as if it were alive.

Our own histories have been written as if this point of view were "other." We thus have great trouble remembering that our view of Earth as a dirt clod was perpetrated on us as children, and on our ancestors, just as it is being perpetrated by our "modern" cultures on "third world" cultures today. As documented by Merlin Stone and Riane Eisler, among others, the Goddess was actually worshiped for thousands of years. We urban peoples are as distanced from the live Earth as people have ever been. But we are also the people whose book learning and psychological sophistication opens us to the Ancient Within and Without as we have never been open before. In this time of great danger and great recovery, we are calling on Her again to help us treasure ourselves and re-enchant our Planet. We are hungry, and She is feeding our souls.

I

All in All: Healing the Split

Out camping a couple of years ago while the sun beat its way around the edge of the day, I lay exhausted on a mat, grateful for the shade provided by the pines above me. Tired and vulnerable as I was, I found myself thinking of those trees as kind, providing me with shade out of their goodness and love. As represented by Eve in the biblical creation story, I had been taught that Nature was beautiful but evil and in need of control. Now, in my involvement with the Goddess, I wanted to reverse that. I wanted to think of Nature as good. But my insistence on understanding Her as one way *or* the other broke on me suddenly. I realized that She is neither good nor evil: She encompasses both those experiences. She is all and nothing. She just *is*.

Earth-centered spirituality is a whole new way of thinking about opposites. In this culture, we are used to dividing the world into good and bad. We think of light as good and dark as bad. High is good; low is bad. The three-part Godhead is all male. It is high in the sky. It represents the Mind, the Word, the Spirit. The Feminine, or what is of the body and the Earth, is low. It is sinful. God the Father is container of all good, and the Christian Devil (whose horned face was borrowed from the ancient Europeans' image of the Goddess's Consort, God of Plenty and Harvest) is container of all evil.

In our patriarchal culture, we are encouraged to split off the parts of ourselves we find fearsome or shameful. We are encouraged to "agree" that anything mysterious or "other" belongs to the "dark" and that dark is bad. Our bodies and their functions are bad. So are our deepest wishes and our "negative" emotions. All must be dominated and controlled by our "lighter," "better," "rational" selves.

What happens to these parts we try to push away? Jungian psychologists call that which we repress the "shadow." They maintain that we tend to "project" our shadows from our insides out. We seem to need a relationship with the whole. When we deny the whole of ourselves or the world, we find other ways to relate to those pushed-away parts. If we are Christians, we may believe also in a Devil, because God the Good Father is only half of the whole. We may find our own disowned selves in women, people of color, children, lesbians, gays, and the natural world itself. We have been trained that what is bad must be disowned; what is disowned then starts looking bad. What is bad in ourselves and others must be dominated and controlled: all those "others" that represent "badness" get a big dose of our efforts to control them.

In Goddess spirituality, we heal the split by committing ourselves to wholeness. We do this by worshiping a Goddess who is both the light and the dark. In order to heal ourselves, our Goddess, our Earth, we must resacralize the dark.

At a Twelve-Step meeting after the October 1989 California earthquake, I listened to a woman struggle with a conversation she had heard between a mother and a small boy. The earthquake and the deaths had been God's will, the mother had explained. "My God doesn't do things like that," said the woman with much emotion. "My God is loving and kind. How can I trust a God who would do something like that?" I could un-

11

derstand that need to believe in the benevolence of the Power greater than ourselves. But I realized that my Goddess *does* do things like that. She *is* the earthquake: She is death; She is sorrow and fear; She is wonder and hope.

How can I be comforted by such an inclusive, even amorphous Greater Power? How can I live with a power that is both Creator and Destroyer; strength and weakness; abundance and famine; terror and comfort?

All great insights are paradoxical. The Goddess as both light and dark is a paradox. If She is dark, how can She be light? If She is light, how can She be dark? That She is both is the mysterious truth. I am comforted by this paradox because it matches my experience of myself and the world. The concept of the Goddess as All in All calls the mystery of life and death by a name I cannot fathom but one that I can know. Even as I tell Her stories, She defies my dissections and definitions. In so doing She touches the awe and wonder that lets me know I am in contact with Her.

Maybe this holding of opposite truths is the basic task of Goddess worship—and of mature adulthood. As adults, we often experience contradictory feelings and know them both to be true. I recognize your loveliness and it is not good for me to be with you. I feel alive and my grief is deep. This brings me pain and it brings me joy.

Just as the Goddess Herself is paradoxical, so is our relationship with Her. When I look at myself in the mirror, I see Carolyn. At the same time, I know that Carolyn embodies more than this image. This is me, and this is not me. I have a similar relationship with the Goddess. On the one hand, I identify with Her. On the other, I dangerously inflate myself when I do not simultaneously identify as Her child, Her worshiper, and as an imperfect human being. Unlike the Goddess, I am a human being who can cultivate but not create a flower; chart but not fill a sea; cut and sew but not mend a body.

I kiss the woman on my left in a Full Moon circle and say, "Thou art Goddess." I mean it; she means it when she passes the kiss and that wonderful statement to the woman beside her.

We giggle at how daring and accurate we are. In the rest of the ritual, we might speak in first person as the Goddess in order to feel Her speaking through us. We identify with Her in order to reclaim the power of the Feminine that our culture has robbed, shunned, and exploited. But, at the same time that we find in Her our personal spiritual identities, we know we are not the All in All.

We are, instead, in relationship with Goddess, internally and externally. We maintain this relationship by seeing Her power and beauty in ourselves and others; making our prayers and meditations tangible through magic; coming together to create sensual theater in Her honor; staring deep into our souls; and moving slowly enough to take in Her grace and wonder.

The inner beliefs, attitudes, and values that instruct our religious path are based on our relationship to the Goddess, within and without. As we explore and practice this relationship, we recognize that we ebb and flow in our ability to feel Her presence and respond to Her. During the heat and flow of relationship, filled with honor and awe for Her presence, choices for right living are clear. For the ebb times in relationship, however, our Earth-centered religion offers a rule. The rule helps us make decisions about behavior even when right attitudes elude us. The only rule of Goddess spirituality is: That which you do comes back to you three times.

When I am using this rule, for example, I will not pour my car oil into the gutter because I do not want to eat petroleum-flavored shrimp in my wonton soup next month. But when I am able to feel my relationship to the Goddess, I am able to move deeper than the rule. I do not pour my oil in the gutter because the sea, the creatures, and I are all One: I operate out of a sense of the sacredness of life rather than fear for my own life.

Goddess-centered morality assumes relationship. It assumes a web of interactions in which no thing is disconnected. Because it reverences the cyclical nature of all things, it assumes that what is spent just takes another form; that we live with the All, even when our minds are tempted to split our actions from their effects.

13

In Goddess spirituality we are not instructed by a series of behavioral commandments. We are instead to struggle with affirming our hopes and dreams in the context of the whole range of our feelings and in clear sight of our own responsibilities and circumstances. If we understand ourselves to live in a reverberating web of life, our actions become mindful. What and how we consume and produce become spiritual concerns. Composting and recycling become religious practices. Respect for Earth and Her Creatures becomes reverence.

Pele (PAY-lay)
Volcano Woman
(Hawaii)

Introduction

P ele is the Goddess who lives in Mount Kilauea on the Hawaiian islands. Goddess of Fire in the Earth, She is Queen
of the wonder and terror evoked by the still-current and lethally
beautiful phenomenon of the Earth's turning inside out. A visitor to Mount Kilauea today may pay a tidy sum for a helicopter
ride over Her steaming mouth.

Early nineteenth-century missionaries encouraged Pele's
people's simultaneous conversion to Christianity and Her des-
ecration through such methods as throwing stones of defiance
into Her crater. As late as the 1950s, however, some Hawaiians
still knew the chants and gifts that would please Her and pe-
tition Her mercy. During more than one volcanic eruption in
that period, proper supplication preceded the cessation of lava
at the edge of several villages.

Mythology has it that the Hawaiian hula began when Pele
asked Her sisters to express delight through dance. To this day

the hula, danced by Hawaiians in the ongoing process of retrieving ancient ways secularized by Christianity and the tourist industry, almost always includes movement sacred to Pele. Powerful chants honor the history of Her wrath, impatience, violence, and Her force in shaping the land. Jealousy and revenge are major themes in Pele's story cycle today, as are the magical potency of music and chanted song in love and romance. From Pele's stories, Hula dancers today derive chants for dance preparation and conversations between lovers or family members. Then—ankles, necks, and foreheads ringed with ferns—they recreate the movements that have doubtless honored the spirits of Earth, Fire, Water, and Air since time out of mind.

In writing Pele's story, I struggled with how to convey the simultaneous accessibility of Pele as Goddess Woman and Her terrible, murderous mystery. My pleas for inspiration to Volcano Woman as I walked and chanted Her name early one Sunday morning were answered in a conversation with the proprietor of the corner store where I had stopped to buy milk. From a small village in India, he told me, his family still worshiped five elements: Fire, Water, Air, Earth, and Metal. And God, he said, was the "Great Balancer of Life and Death." With this luminous phrase, the how-and-why love tale of Pele was set suddenly like a jewel in a ring, and I went home to write.

Pele's stone is obsidian and Her colors are red and black. Pele has helped me accept the force of my own feelings and to live with questions about natural tragedy.

The Romance of Volcano and Ocean

HEN THE CEN-
ter of the Earth swells red hot and roars to meet the sky and
rivers of fire race down the mountain, the people cry in terror.
Even the old ones who know the name of Volcano Woman
bring Her presents of silk and tobacco with their knees trembling. At the edge of Her mouth they set their gifts, and though
Her steaming cry does not sound like She is grateful, more than
once Her liquid fire has stopped at the edge of the village and
the people and their animals are left alive.

Pele is the name of Volcano Woman, and no one really
knows why She comes from the center of the Earth dressed in
Her terrible beauty.

Some people say it is not really Pele that comes from the
center, but Her children instead. Long ago, they say, when Pele
was young, the center of the Earth glowed with Her loveliness.
Her skin was black as coal and Her hair red as flames. Singing

17

Her song that hissed like steam through a small opening, She was content for a million years to putter in Her house, stirring Her red pepper soup in Her huge iron pot. Sometimes She would sleep for a hundred years at a time, Her arms wrapped around Her brown and yellow snakes.

Then one day, Pele walked to the edge of the center and pushed Her hands upward. That was the day Pele met Ocean. For in pushing upward, Pele made a crack in the center, and through the crack came Ocean's voice, deep and soft. "Pele, may I come in?" asked Ocean. Pele drew back. "I don't know you," She said. "Then let us meet here again and again and talk until we do know each other," said Ocean.

That was how the conversations began. For a thousand years, Pele came to the crack and talked with Ocean. Some days Ocean didn't answer Her call. But She could hear his voice boiling and dark in the distance. And some days Pele didn't come at Ocean's call. But every day they did talk, Pele's heart swelled with curiosity and wonder. For Ocean asked Her about Her soup and Her snakes. He asked Her what She dreamed when She slept. He asked Her about the shapes of Her rocks. Ocean told Her about his wet purple world. He told Her about the color green, and he told Her about the sky. One day, Pele whispered to Ocean that She loved him.

"Oh, my Pele," said Ocean. "My wonderful friend," said Ocean. "Will you let me come in now?"

Pele felt Her skin prickle. "Ocean, I am afraid," She said. But She curled Her fingers into the edges of the crack and pulled. Her muscles rippled and the crack opened wide. Ocean fell into Her arms.

That was the beginning, the people say, of the marriage of Pele and Ocean. Some say it is when Pele is fighting with Her husband that the volcano bursts. Others say that lava is the offspring of Pele and Ocean. It is the fire of Pele that makes the lava red hot, and the water of Ocean that makes it flow like a mighty river.

But some of the old ones shake their heads. No one knows

18

the Volcano Woman, they say—not even Ocean. The volcano explodes only when Pele comes up from the center to balance the great scale of life and death. The Volcano Woman is the Great Balancer, they say. But that is another story.

Amaterasu Omikami
(ah-mah-ter-RAH-su
oh-mee-KAH-mee)
She Who Possesses Noon
(Japan)

Introduction

The eight-armed mirror of the Sun Goddess Amaterasu Omikami can be seen to this day in the Shinto shrine near the town of Uji Yamada by the Ise River in Japan. The Shinto religion, widespread in Japan today, is a synthesis of deep nature reverence and the political belief that Japan's royal family derives its heritage from the Divine Ancestress Herself: Amaterasu Omikami. Perhaps the eight arms of the mirror are reminiscent of a sea creature like the octopus that ancients may once have imagined to hold up their many-islanded world. Speculate we can; ascertain we cannot. For written records of Amaterasu's story begin in the eighth century of this Common Era along with all the other records of ancient Japan.

The *Kojiki* and the *Nihongi*, commissioned in 712 C.E.,* pro-

*The abbreviation C.E. stands for Common Era, equivalent to the use of A.D. Before the Common Era is denoted by the letters B.C.E., equivalent to the use of B.C.

20

vide keys to understanding Japanese mythology. While both honor Amaterasu as a major deity, accounts of Her origin differ (in much the same way that biblical Gospel accounts of the life of Jesus vary), and the texts show clear patriarchal biases as well. We also know that eighth-century scribes intentionally synthesized two bodies of belief and imagery: Buddhist and Shinto. In both texts, however, Amaterasu speaks of Izanami as Her Mother. The ancient Izanami may well have been a great Serpent of the Sea, responsible for the formation of land and life. Her Daughter, Amaterasu, was born from Her eye.

Amaterasu's story is my version of the myth of the Sun Goddess and Her Brother Susanowo (sue-sah-NO-woe), Ruler of the Ocean, told in Merlin Stone's *Ancient Mirrors of Womanhood*. The myth perhaps reenacts the tenuous nature of the annual rice-growing cycle on an island world at the mercy of the sea. Then too, the Winter Solstice of every year parallels the time when Amaterasu Omikami shuts Herself away in Her cave. The tree beside the Ise River shrine is hung, to this day, with jewels and mirrors to attract Her returning light.

The *kami* of Amaterasu's second name, Omikami, is defined as spiritual essence. Shinto worshipers honor the living *kami* in each part of the natural environment. Though the word *omi* in Japanese has no particular meaning, aside from being the Goddess's appellation, its similarity to the prefix *omni* helps us to understand Amaterasu's all-inclusiveness more deeply.

Amaterasu Omikami's symbols are the mirror and rice. I have called on Amaterasu at Winter Solstice and at times when a quality nurtured in the cave of myself needs to emerge. Because Her story in this collection deals with Her Brother's drunkenness, it has also inspired reflection about my response to substance abuse in others.

Japan is one of several cultures whose peoples know the Sun Deity as Female. Other cultures include the Arunta of Australia (see the story of Sun Woman); the Tobu of Argentina; the Inuit of Siberia, Alaska, Northern Canada, and Greenland; people of ancient Arabia; and people of Anatolia (Turkey).

The Mirror Dance of Life

N O ONE IS ALIVE
anymore who can remember the time Amaterasu Omikami, the
Great Woman Who Possesses Noon, took Herself into the Cave
of Heaven and refused to come out. But to those who know the
story, every mirror on Earth is a reminder of that time and of
the glorious moment She stepped again into the open sky, send-
ing Her surge of strength and will again through all Life.

In those beginning times, the spirit of every living thing was
called its Kami. The Kami of the mountain was lavender and
long. The Kami of the trees was great and green. Animals had
Kami in the shapes of swords and cups. Fish and flowers had
Kami. The Kami of the rocks and the rivers were silent and
calm. All the strength of these Kami poured forth from the
Great Mother Sun, Amaterasu Omikami, and in Her honor was
woven the great pattern of the seasons of the planting and the
harvesting of rice.

Amaterasu Omikami had a Brother named Susanowo. Susanowo ruled the ocean, but He was jealous of the greater power of His Sister, Amaterasu. Because Amaterasu knew of His ill feeling, She was suspicious when one day Susanowo sent word that He was coming to visit. Though She had a feast prepared on the day Her Brother was to arrive, Amaterasu also armed Herself with a quiver of ten thousand silver arrows and a giant bow of beaten gold. She planted Her feet firmly and awaited Susanowo.

Some of the Queen of Heaven's tension melted when She saw that Susanowo came bearing gifts and speaking of trust and loyalty. Amaterasu and Susanowo ate together, and, after the meal had been cleared away, Amaterasu covered Her Brother's hands with Her own. "How glad I am You've come in friendship," said Amaterasu, Her eyes shining. "I was worried You'd come otherwise."

Susanowo loosed His hands and bowed low to His Sister. "Amaterasu Omikami," He said. "Let Us forget the past. I have nothing but respect and admiration for You."

Late into the night They talked of Their love for each other, Their plans for the future, and the joy of Their relationship. Finally Amaterasu bid Susanowo good night and went to Her cave to sleep.

Susanowo, however, did not go to bed. Instead He sat alone at the huge table, sipping sake wine and growing increasingly angry as He compared His own power to that of His Sister. The memory of the food, conversation, and Amaterasu's graciousness grew ugly in Susanowo's mind. The wine He was drinking slowly kindled His resolve to show His Sister who was really most powerful.

In the next few hours, Susanowo tore drunkenly through the Plain of Heaven. He piled mounds of dirt in the irrigation canals so no water could flow to the rice paddies. Not satisfied, He stomped on each and every plant until the fields were covered with broken and dying stalks. Then He took up the excrement of animals and humans and smeared it in Amaterasu's celestial weaving house where the heavenly women wove the sacred tapestries.

In fear and anger, the Gods and Goddesses went to wake Amaterasu. When the Shining One saw what Her Brother had done, a pain stabbed Her heart. Her hands hung limp at Her sides, and Her mind pictured the dinner they had shared and the words of trust and endearment They had exchanged.

"Susanowo!" Amaterasu's voice filled the Plain of Heaven like light suddenly fills a dark room.

Susanowo staggered into His Sister's presence, pulling a piebald colt on a rope behind Him. He spat on the floor of the celestial palace.

Amaterasu put Her hands behind Her back. "Susanowo," She said again. "Where are the words of last night, Susanowo?"

Susanowo spat again.

"Susanowo," said Amaterasu again. "Susanowo, You wrong Me. But I ask only that You sleep. Leave off, Brother Susanowo. Sleep."

Susanowo answered by pulling the sword from His belt and whirling to plunge its blade through the heart of the colt behind Him. Before the eyes of the entire heavenly court, He heaved the dead colt through the window of the palace and into the celestial weaving house below. There the carcass struck and broke the looms and sacred threads and sent several of the heavenly weavers to the Land of the Dead.

A cry of rage escaped the throat of Amaterasu Omikami. She ran from the palace and back to Her cave. Once inside, She pulled the great door tight behind Her and locked it, shutting away from Heaven Her warmth and light and plunging even the realm of Susanowo into darkness.

The Gods and Goddesses of Heaven caught Susanowo, punished Him, and banished Him from Heaven. But without Amaterasu Omikami to light the Plain of Heaven, there was only darkness. The Kami of the rice withered. The Kami of birds and animals, mountains and trees turned to gray ghosts. Life without Amaterasu Omikami was impossible.

The Gods and Goddesses gathered together to discuss how they might restore the precious Amaterasu Omikami. How to tempt Her from Her cave? How to let Her know that Susanowo had been sent away?

"We must moan and grieve outside Her cave. We must shout to Her of our dead," said some of the deities. "No," said others. "We must remind Her of the joy She brings. We must dance for Her."

And so it was that the Dance of the Mirrors was planned. All of the ghostly Kami of the world gathered up what little strength they had left and pieces of shiny mirror. With the help of the Gods and Goddesses, they collected themselves outside the door of Amaterasu's cave and began to make a joyful noise. Songs and jokes flew, weakly at first and then, as the Kami began to take strength from each other, more strongly. A dance bloomed, and deep inside the Cave of Heaven Amaterasu Omikami heard the voices of Her people.

When Amaterasu cracked open the door of Her cave, a slit of Her brilliant light lit the night. When the Kami felt the surge of Life they had longed for, the dance became jubilant. Amaterasu listened and then poked Her head outside the cave. At that very moment the mirrors of all the Kami reflected back to Amaterasu Omikami Her own stunning beauty, and Amaterasu Omikami stepped all the way out of Her cave and into the open sky.

Once again the Kami of the mountain grew lavender and long. The Kami of the trees was once again great and green. Animals again had Kami in the shapes of swords and cups. The Kami of fish and flowers and rocks and rivers were alive once more.

On that day the strength of all Kami poured forth from the Great Mother Sun, and in Her honor was woven the great pattern of the seasons of the planting and the harvesting of rice. And so it is to this very day.

Ereshkigal (uh-RESH-kig-gull)
Queen of the Underworld
and
Inanna (ee-NAH-nah)
Queen of Heaven
(Middle East)

Introduction

C hristian storytellers borrowed extensively from the myth of Ereshkigal and Her Sister Inanna when they put together the story of the crucifixion and resurrection of Jesus. Indeed, it was Inanna, Queen of Heaven, who first taught Her people how to die, be reborn, and rise again.

The stories of Inanna and Ereshkigal are recorded on cuneiform tablets dating up to 3200 years before the birth of Christ. They come from Sumer, the most ancient literate civilization we know, today's Iraq and Middle East. Our knowledge of ancient Sumer is pieced together from the findings and interpretations of archaeologists and scholars, and Sumer's artifacts are still being discovered. These writings reveal the tremendous power of the Goddess and Her worship over time, as well as dramatic accounts of Her conquer and the resulting emotional devastation of Herself and Her people.

Ereshkigal is the older of the two Goddesses: Her name appears in the oldest of Sumer's writings. She is Queen of Irkalla, the Land of the Dead; Queen of Souls; the Most Merciful One. Her name *Kigal* means "Great Earth." Her counterparts in other cultures include Nephthys of Egypt; Persephone of Greece (see story); Kali of India (see story); and Hel of northern Europe, whose name Christian storytellers borrowed for the Underworld they called hell.

Inanna, whose Holy Lap was the source of the Earth's life blood (see story of Danu) in the form of wells, rivers, and springs, was the most widely known Goddess in later Sumerian history. Queen of Heaven, She was Venus, the Morning and Evening Stars, and was represented by an eight-petaled star or rosette. (Both Amaterasu Omikami of Japan and Iamanja of Brazil are similarly associated: see stories.) Her animal counterparts were the snake, coiled on a staff, and the heifer, whose horns most probably represented the shapes of the Moon and the sacred Fallopian Tubes of life. She is related to the Semitic Goddess Ishtar and probably descended from the Creator Goddess Nammu, who was Herself associated with the Mesopotamian Tiamat. The story of Tiamat, Great Mother of the Sea, finally recounts Her murder at the hands of male invaders.

As the myth of Amaterasu Omikami is a metaphor for the rice-growing cycle, the story of Inanna's descent and return from Her Sister Ereshkigal probably dramatizes the seasonal shift between the time of rain and plenty and the frightening time of drought and possible famine. The story of the seasons is perhaps the deepest one we humans know. It is no accident that Christian tellers who mapped for us the story of their Jesus pinpointed His return to life in the Spring of the northern hemisphere. And, like the figure of Jesus, the Sumerian Sister Goddesses in that far earlier version of this tremendous story of death and renewal touch deeply the seasonal nature of our own personal psychologies.

I have invoked Inanna and Ereshkigal with bones, seeds,

pits, and compost. I have called on the Sisters for help with grief, terror, loss, and recovery. Ereshkigal embodies my ability to let truth be, without trying to fix or change it. Inanna embodies hope and the courage to change.

To Die, Be Reborn, and Rise Again

OON AFTER THE Goddess Inanna, Queen of Heaven, took for Herself the human Dumuzi as Her husband, She heard that the husband of Her Sister Ereshkigal, Queen of the Underworld, had died.

Inanna decided to go to Ereshkigal and be with Her Sister in the Underworld as She mourned. But when She called to Her friend and helper Ninshubar to help Her dress for Her journey, she got an argument instead.

"Don't go," said Ninshubar. "Please, my Queen. Send Your Sister Your sympathy by messenger."

"Ninshubar," said Inanna. "A message is not the same as My presence. I need to go to Her."

"Beloved Inanna," said Ninshubar. "Ereshkigal sent You a message. You can send Her one. I'm afraid She is Queen of a realm that will exact from You everything You have if You go. Inanna. Please. It is dangerous to go to Ereshkigal's Underworld. Inanna, the guards will take Your fine garments. They will exact a price from You, Inanna. They may take Your life."

"Ninshubar, I am going to go," said Inanna. "But I can see how worried you are, and so I concede this one thing. If I do not return in three days, send someone after me."

And so it was agreed. Ninshubar helped Inanna dress in garments that best proclaimed Her Queen of Heaven. The starry velvet train of Her gown floated after Her as She and Her servants left the Realm of Heaven and made their way to the Underworld.

At the opening to the Underworld, Inanna left Her servants. "This journey I take alone," She told them, and began Her way down to the palace of Her Sister.

When She had walked the first thousand steps into the Earth, She came to the first gate. She could not see the faces of the guards there, but She could hear their voices. "Give us Your crown," they ordered.

"Do you know to Whom you speak?" said Inanna.

"We know," said the voices. "There is no passage here without a price. Give up Your crown."

Inanna lifted the golden crown from Her head and gave it to the guards. The gate opened.

Inanna descended another thousand steps. There was no light now, other than the light of Her own self. She came to the second gate. Here the guards asked for Her earrings.

"I do not plan to stay," said Inanna. "I am a visitor here only."

"Ereshkigal exacts payment from everyone who enters here. Even visitors," said the guards.

Inanna unhooked the jewels from Her lobes. She gave them to the guards. The second gate opened.

At the third gate, Inanna had to give over Her necklace. It weighed heavily in Her hands as She passed it to the guards. The gate opened.

Inanna traveled another thousand steps deep. There they took Her cloak with its starry velvet train. She shivered with cold. The fourth gate opened.

At the fifth gate, the guards asked Inanna for Her diamond belt. Inanna held Her head proudly, but Her voice trembled. "You have taken My crown and all of My jewels. You have stripped the covering from My shoulders and chest. Surely that is enough. You will not also take the belt that holds up My skirts?"

"The price of entering here is Your belt," said the guards in voices that had no trembling. Inanna gave over Her belt and held up Her skirts with Her hands.

At the sixth gate, Inanna said, "I am naked without My skirt."

"You must give up Your skirt," said the guards.

Inanna wrapped Her arms about Herself for warmth and comfort. Her skirt fell to the floor, and She stepped away from it. The gate opened.

"This is the last gate," said the guards at the seventh gate. "To enter here, Inanna, Queen of Heaven, You must give up Your last."

Inanna used Her right foot to push the jeweled shoe from Her left foot. But the toes of Her bare left foot could not push off Her right shoe. So Inanna bent and with both hands removed that last bit of covering from Her body. The floor was icy cold. The last gate opened, and Inanna passed into the palace of the Queen of the Underworld.

There sat Ereshkigal on Her throne. Her face was turned away from the door. Her hands lay limp on Her knees. Inanna saw that the ceiling of the huge dark room curved over absolutely nothing except Her Sister on Her throne, the coffin before Her, and a basin of blood.

"Sister!" whispered Inanna.

The word echoed in the emptiness. "Sister!" said Inanna, louder this time. Her voice sounded little and afraid.

Slowly Ereshkigal turned Her face away from the shadows. Only Her neck moved. The Goddess's body on Her throne stayed still.

Inanna walked forward in the cold with Her hands outstretched. "Sister," She said. There were tears on Her face.

31

Inanna stopped when Her eyes met the eyes of Ereshkigal. Ereshkigal's face did not move. Inanna saw that in the center of each of Her Sister's eyes was a tiny human skull. Each of the skulls had eyes. All the eyes stared at Inanna.

Inanna fell to Her knees. "Sister!" She cried. "You do not greet Me and I have come to comfort You! Sister, greet Me! Let Me mourn with You."

The terrible eyes of Ereshkigal didn't answer. They just looked.

"Ereshkigal!" cried Inanna. "Don't You know Me? I am Your Sister!"

The mouth of Ereshkigal opened. "I know You," She said. Her voice was flat. "You are My Sister, Inanna, Queen of Heaven, and You've come here to die."

"I've come to help You mourn, Ereshkigal. Not to die! To mourn! To cry with You. To hold You. Ereshkigal! Stop looking at Me!"

Ereshkigal had moved Her hands to the arms of Her throne. Her fingers had curled in strength there and were pushing Her body forward. Her eyes with the skulls in them seemed to pierce through Inanna. "No one escapes this House of Death, Inanna. No one. You die, Inanna."

Inanna began to rock forward and backward. Her shoulders shook. Her neck arched. She tried to wrench Her face away from the face of Her Sister. But Her head was held in the force of the Queen of the Underworld's eyes. With a terrible noise, Inanna died.

Ereshkigal picked up the body of Her Sister in Her arms and carried it to the wall. There on a giant hook She hung it and went back to sit on Her throne.

Three days had passed back in the palace of the Queen of Heaven. Inanna had not returned. Ninshubar tied a knife to her belt under her skirts and went for help. She went first to one God, and then another. Both refused to help.

Ninshubar began to run. Panting, she came to the house of Enkil. "Enkil," she gasped. "Inanna has not returned from Ereshkigal. Please help."

Enkil was immediately alert. He poured Ninshubar a glass of cool water and bade her drink and rest. Ninshubar swallowed thirstily and began to breathe more easily.

"There!" Enkil smiled. "Now for help." He sat quietly for some moments and then looked at His hands. "Aha!" He said. "I know just the thing!" From under His little fingernail He flicked two specks of dirt. He set them on the end of His index finger and blew them into the air. At once the two bits of dirt changed to two tiny demons with pointed ears, feet, and tongues. "Off with you both to the Underworld," said Enkil. "Come back with our Queen Inanna."

The demons flew off on their tiny wings. Down they went, so small and quick that the guards at the seven gates did not even notice them as they darted through each gate's latticework.

In the throne room of Ereshkigal the demons saw a terrible sight. Queen Inanna hung rotting on a hook. Flies buzzed around Her body. The basin of blood had spilled, and Queen Ereshkigal was hanging over the edge of the coffin at the center of the room moaning and screaming in pain and grief. The demons touched hands for a moment and then flew to each side of the sobbing Queen.

"My husband is dead!" screamed Ereshkigal.

"Your husband is dead, O Queen," sang the demons.

"My husband is dead. My Sister is dead. I am lower than low," moaned Ereshkigal.

"Your husband is dead. Your Sister is dead. You are lower than low, O Queen," sang the demons.

"I am lower than low. My stomach crawls on the floor," moaned Ereshkigal.

"You are lower than low. Your stomach crawls on the floor," sang the demons.

Ereshkigal sobbed for a long time. The demons hovered quietly. For another long time, Ereshkigal lay quiet. Finally,

She raised Her head and looked at the demons. Her eyes were wet and deep, but there were no skulls in them now.

"Who are you?" asked Ereshkigal.

"We've come for Queen Inanna," sang the demons.

Ereshkigal hiccuped. "Your song is good, small ones," said Ereshkigal. "Help Me take Her down."

Ereshkigal and the demons lifted Inanna's body from the horrible hook.

"We have died together, My Sister and I," said Ereshkigal. "It is the law of the Underworld."

"Tell us the law, Queen Ereshkigal," sang the demons.

"My Sister leaves. But the law is that She must send another in Her place," said Ereshkigal.

"She must send another in Her place," sang the demons. "That is the law."

So they took Queen Inanna's body back up through the seven gates. At each gate, the guards gave back Inanna's garments.

Then, at the opening to the Upper World, the demons waited and watched as Inanna revived Herself. Awake and whole finally, She stood, and the demons bathed Her and fed Her. And when they had dressed Her in all Her finery, they told Her Ereshkigal's instructions. "You must send someone down, O Queen, to take Your place," they sang and flew away.

Inanna opened Her arms to the trees and the sky and stepped one giant step into Her palace. At the first archway, She met Her Brother, crying bitterly for the loss of His Sister. "Brother," said Inanna, "do not grieve. I am here! I have returned. Dance with Me for joy."

At the second archway, Inanna met Her Son, smearing His face with ashes for the loss of His Mother. "My Son, do not grieve," said Inanna. "I am back! I have returned! Dance with Me for joy."

Then Inanna saw Ninshubar. She took Her friend in Her arms and held her close.

"You have returned, my Queen," said Ninshubar.

"Where is My husband?" said Inanna. "I long for him. Where is he?"

Ninshubar looked away and shook her head.

"Ninshubar! Where is My husband?" said Inanna. "I will go to him in the fields with his sheep. How I long to be in his arms!"

"Inanna," said Ninshubar. "Dumuzi is not in his field."

"Where is he then?" asked Inanna.

"He is in Your throne room," answered Ninshubar.

Inanna picked up Her skirts and ran to the center of Her palace. There on Her throne She saw Her husband. But Dumuzi was not crying. Nor was his face smeared with ashes. Instead Dumuzi was laughing and ordering the musicians to play another round of music. "Eat, drink, and be merry!" he shouted to the party of people. "I am king!"

Dumuzi stopped short when he saw his Queen. Inanna's face had frozen hard. She stood very still.

"Inanna!" said Dumuzi. "You have returned! Inanna, I . . . ."

Inanna pointed Her finger at Dumuzi. "You," She said. "You. It is you who shall take My place with Ereshkigal."

The blood ran out of Dumuzi's face. "My Queen," he said.

"Queen Inanna!" A woman ran out of the crowd and knelt at Inanna's feet. "You know me. I am Geshtinanna, Dumuzi's sister. We were wrong not to grieve You, O Queen. But Inanna, we are human, and life seemed so short. We have danced and made merry today because we could die tomorrow. We were afraid, Inanna. O Queen Inanna, show mercy to me and my brother. Let us share the time in the Underworld."

Inanna looked at Geshtinanna and then at Dumuzi. "So be it," said the Queen of Heaven, and She turned away.

So it is that half the year Dumuzi the shepherd spends tending his sheep while his sister lives in the Underworld. The other half of the year Dumuzi lives in the realm of Ereshkigal while his sister, Geshtinanna, lives in the Upper World. Each year the brother and sister pass on the staircase of the seven gates and hold each other tightly before they separate again.

Hecate (HEK-uh-tay)
Queen of the Crossroads
(Turkey)

Introduction

Worshiped in both Greece and Anatolia, or ancient Turkey, the Dark Goddess Hecate was related to the Goddess Hekat of the ancient Nubian people, the black-skinned rulers and people of Egypt. Hekat, Oldest of the Old, swam in water and walked on dry land. She was the magical essence of Au Set, the Mighty Mother of Transformation, called Isis by the Greeks (see story).

Hecate was Goddess of the Amazons, the Greek name for the Mother-worshiping nomadic tribes of women in North Africa, Anatolia, and the area near the Black Sea. Led by Hecate, Commander of the Mother's Words of Power, this fabled group of people once ruled over large parts of Asia. They may have been the first people to tame horses, and they were known for their physical and magical capacities to wage war. The name Amazon probably meant "Moon Woman," and some colonies of Amazons were said to live on women-only islands (such as Taurus, Lemnos, and Lesbos), consorting with males only when they wanted to conceive children.

Hecate's images and Her magic cauldron were placed at threefold road crossings. For centuries Her peoples invoked Her protection when they traveled and left gifts at Her road shrines on nights of the Full Moon. Her sacred hounds were said to bay hymns to Her when She appeared.

Greeks associated their Hecate with both Persephone of the Underworld (see story) and the dark side of the Goddess Artemis: when the waxing Huntress Moon disappeared, the Crone energy of Hecate was said to take Her place.

The European Middle Ages diabolized Hecate as Queen of Ghosts and Witches. Catholic authorities said midwives, who were Her wise women, were most dangerous to the Christian faith.

I wrote Hecate's story in order to present the erased and abused aspect of Goddess as Crone in a way that might begin to heal Her image for myself and others. We know of no Crone more ancient than Earth Herself, and some of my ability to be in relationship with the Great Wrinkled One depends on my relationship with human aging.

Offerings of bread or cake can be made to the Queen of the Crossroads for Her protection for travel. Figuratively, Hecate is also Queen of Crossroads in mature living, in which choices are rarely either-or, black or white, but of varied and subtle grays. Hecate has helped me find kindliness in my own agony of decision making and to let go of that which I must in order to move on. She can be invoked during the waning or dark of the Moon with a bit of fur combed from a black dog.

The Woman Behind the Door
of the Moon

N A DARK
Halloween night a long time ago the sea was deep and black under the cape of the sky. The waves swelled shimmery green and crashed on the shore. Then something else began to swell beneath the waters. Thirteen silver fish boiled up to the surface of the sea and flipped onto the land. The fish panted on the sand, and the moon slipped into the sky from behind a cloud.

That was when the thirteen silver fish changed to thirteen huge black dogs. The dogs leapt at the moon and then began to run. They hurtled across the beach and onto the road where they ran and ran until they came to the place where the road crossed with two others.

And there at the road crossing, the dogs began to chase each other clockwise under the light of the moon. Out of the blur of fur and black came something else.

Not fish, not dogs. This time girls. Women. Mothers. Cousins. Daughters. Nieces. Aunts. Grandmothers and granddaughters. Friends. All of them dancing and stepping high under the moon.

"Hecate!" the people shouted. "Hecate!" they whispered. "Lady! Come to us!" They tipped their heads back and called to the moon. Called to the round white circle in the black velvet sky. "Mother! Hecate! Come to us!"

A door opened. Up in the moon, a door opened. The people on the ground below breathed. A ladder came out of the door. Rung after rung, it slipped through the sky. Finally it reached the ground at the center of the circle. While the people in the circle looked up, a figure emerged from the door in the moon and began to climb down the ladder.

The figure came closer and closer. And the people in the circle below began to see it was a Woman. Hooded and hunched. With a huge bag slung over Her robes. Down, down She traveled, until finally She stood in the center of the people.

With both gnarled hands She heaved the bag off Her shoulder. Then She removed the hood from Her head. A little girl said, "You're here!"

The Old Woman's face smiled. The moon lit the creases of Her skin and the white mane of Her hair. She opened the bag.

Inside were glasses of milk foaming just at the brims and chocolate chip cookies with raisins and almonds. For eating and eating and eating. The girls ate. The mothers ate. The friends and the cousins and the grandmothers ate. The aunts and the nieces ate; the granddaughters ate. They ate until they were full.

Then the Old Woman closed Her bag. And She climbed back into the sky. She pulled up Her ladder. And She closed the door. The moon glowed.

The women below began to dance. Faster and faster they moved. A circle of light. Whirling round and round. And then black. Furry and black. Thirteen dogs, howling at the moon. Then running. Bounding and leaping together. Away from the crossroads. Away down the road. Back across the beach. Then panting at the edge of the sea. Panting and panting. Panting silver fish. Thirteen silver fish on the sand.

Then a flinging of those fish bodies into the sea. The sea deep and dark under the cape of the sky. That's how it was on a Halloween night a long, long time ago.

Constant Change:
The Everlasting Cycle

Thin greens glove the buds on the narcissus plant. Now the gloves turn brown and shrivel. They are dying in order to free the blossoms.

Earth-centered spirituality honors as sacred this circular pattern of death to life to death and life again. Death is not a punishment from the Goddess: it is instead the culmination of a process that endlessly repeats itself on the smallest and largest scales. Paradoxically, the power of the universe that is essentially *being* is also in constant flux. Her patterns of light are born and disappear over the course of a day; She moves from evening to night, from dawn to morning. The baby becomes a boy; the girl begins to menstruate; the friend does not come through; the career shift is made; we lose the fantasy and adapt to the reality.

The Goddess's one constant is change. Her lore mythologizes Her perennial shape shifting in wonderful ways. When She is portrayed as the Sun, Her changes can be understood as the yearly changes that send us deep into winter caves and find us dancing on summer mountains. When She is the Moon, she is understood as continuously merging into different phases of Herself: She is New and Waxing large; She is Full; and She is Waning and Dark. As the Moon, She has three faces: Maiden, Mother, Crone.

As the New and Waxing Moon, She is Maiden or Virgin. Her territory is Herself. She strides the night of Her soul free and clear of other than self-commitment. Even when She is relational and sexual with others, Her knowing comes from the pool She gazes into alone. The Virgin turns corners and travels new paths. She fiercely protects the child. The Virgin is Creator. Out of nothingness, She brings forth Herself. This is the time for wishes to take the form of affirmations and for affirmations to take action.

As the Full Moon, She is Mother, Preserver, Realizer; Her territory is transition. She is Keeper of the Mundane. Unlike the focused attention of the Virgin, the Mother's attention is diffuse and contains the whole picture. She is knitting, laughing, talking, and baking all at once. She is abundance. She is the luminous center of the Cycle that has begun in nothing and will end in darkness. This is the time for stock taking, stock making, for rejoicing, feasting, and being in the complexity of the webs of our lives.

As the Old One, as the Waning Moon, She is the Crone, the Ancient Ender. She has birthed and buried the loves of Her heart; She has killed what needed killing. She has sat with the doomed and the usual and can let the child sob on Her lap. She tells the truth; She is the Undertaker of Dreams; disillusion is Her realm. Now is the time to let it come apart, to let go of what we once were sure we could not live without.

Everything on Earth instructs us about Her everlasting, cyclical change. We take in through our mouths and let go through our anuses, over and over again. Our hormones peak and drop daily and monthly, manifesting energy levels and moods. Our relationships ebb and flow. Sometimes we are productive and inspired; sometimes we lie tiny and fallow. Our gardens poke up enchantingly; they fill rebelliously with weeds;

they fashion full plants for our tables; they lie rotting and dense until we begin again. Days pass in sets of seven; months curve around us and turn into years. Workplaces shift personnel, customers, products; establishments become memories and certainties only photographs. The once young are now elders; the once little are now feeding and diapering their own. Waves of politics come and go. Departures, tornadoes, thefts, and divorces smash our hopes, undo our routines, leave us stunned, panting, and simple to begin again.

Anyone who has chanted knows that chanting past the point of boredom deepens the imprint and power of this kind of music making. Anyone who has stared from the edge of a cliff at the waves below knows the peace that comes with endless crashings and silences. How comforted we humans are with the table set the same way for the holiday, the story told for the twentieth time, the line quadrupled in the poem. Our deepest rhythms are cyclical and repetitive. In Goddess spirituality, we view these returns as rhythms of the Goddess. We call the Cycle sacred. Although our culture has great difficulty honoring death, depression, and despair, we humans pass our lives unable to avoid the endings that make way for beginnings. As we mature and deepen, we learn to hold the completions as sacred as the starts.

We humans are able finally to accept the endings in the context of the Cycle. Our rituals therefore are circular: we sit in circles, we create beginnings, middles, and ends, and we promise each other we will meet again. Like the ancients, we set our rituals in the context of the cyclical year. As far away as we live from the beat of agricultural life, Goddess worshipers can still comprehend at least eight points in the turning of the Great Wheel of Life. Outside and inside, our year begins, like Life itself, in the dark. In the northern hemisphere, Halloween (October 31/November 1) is our New Year. Like a seed in the ground or a fetus in the womb, our hope and joy are born of the dark. At New Year the veil is very thin between what has been and what will be in our lives. Winter Solstice (December 21) heralds light's birth; inside our caves we nurture ourselves. At Candlemas (February 1), we emerge from our caves carrying the lights of the early blossoms and the plans we are making. Spring Equinox (March 21) honors the sassy and confusing puberties of our projects and ourselves. Beltaine (May 1) couples us and all things with the force of Life. At Summer Solstice (June 21), the longest and the strongest of the light, we are overflowing with concerted effort. On Lammas Day (August 1), even we supermarket customers take the time to honor the abundant fruits of the farmer's labor and our own. At Fall Equinox (September 21), we watch the yellowness of the light turn milky in the cooling air. It is time for self-assessment. We are beginning to move into the dark that will start the Cycle once more.

Nothing we plan, say, or do has any effect on these great changes. Earth turns always, travels Her orbit, and carries us with Her. Perhaps we singing, moving, meditating creatures are Earth's consciousness. Perhaps it is through the emotional perceptions and expression of Her humans that She registers Her awesome wonder and sorrow. As keeper of Her sacredness, we worship Her great process out of which we come and to which always we return.

Danu (DAN-oo)
The Earth
(Ireland)

Introduction

Despite increasing industrialization, today's Ireland is famed for her still-told stories of fairy mounds and little people in the grass. Today's tales are Earth-respecting remnants of the sagas of human-sized, magically powered queens, kings, heroes, and heroines that preceded them. These stories, in turn, recapitulate the even older tales when Goddesses and Gods, representing the powers of Earth, Water, Fire, and Air, peopled the world. The tellers of those ancient stories called themselves the Tuatha De Danaan, or the "Tribe of the Goddess Danu."

The Irish Danu, Danuna, or Dana shared Her name with forms of the Great Mother in cultures around the world, such as the Danes and the biblical Danites (called "serpents" by writers of the Old Testament). The Russians called Her Dennitsa (see the story of the Zoryas); the classical Greeks named Her Danae; the Hebrews Dinah; and the Babylonians called Her Danu or Dunnu.

46

Although the ancient Tuatha De Danaan named the Earth Goddess as the very source of their lives, Danu is rarely mentioned by today's authors trying to piece together the myths from that time. Instead, most stories told today emphasize the role of Dagdu, the Sun God. A traveler to County Meath in Ireland can, for example, visit Newgrange, a beautifully preserved tomb built in the form of an underground temple in 3000 B.C.E.—or five hundred years before the erection of the pyramids. The entrance stones are inscribed with giant spirals, and the damp, cool passageway to the center is now rigged electrically to expose spirals and inverted triangles etched on the inner walls. The guide also uses an electric light to reenact the nearly miraculous once-a-year flooding of the dark center (through the window in the roof) with the light of the rising Sun on the morning of the Winter Solstice. The sense of being in a womblike place is overwhelming. The literature provided to Newgrange visitors, however, fails to note this obvious reality. Instead, it first praises the high degree of architectural, engineering, and artistic skill displayed by this ancient crop-raising people and carefully notes the measurements and placement of roofbox, chambers, great circle, and surrounding standing stones of the Great Mound. The pamphlet's author then declares that Newgrange is a monument to "no less a personage than the chief of all the gods," Dagdu the Sun.

I wrote the story of Danu the Earth after a moving visit to this underground temple. Unlike the pamphlet's author, I had to ask myself why a people would build a monument to the Sun inside the Earth in such a way as to take the light of the Sun into its depths for only minutes each year.

I was further inspired by my visit to the bowels of Dublin's museum in which are gathered a dozen or so of what curators call "sheila-na-gigs." Sheila-na-gigs are stone figures of squatting women displaying their sometimes red-stained vulvas. As late as the Middle Ages, these figures were carved above church entryways. Both the churches and their startling guardians were built by medieval Goddess-worshiping villagers in the process of capitulating to the Christian religion.

47

Danu, I have no doubt, was a figure much like the far more modern sheila-na-gigs, who almost certainly represented the womb and tomb as the single point at which meet life and death in the Cycle of the Great Mother.

In Danu's story, I hope to spiral through time to the very center of our own stories. It is the story of Danu's filling the world with Her rhythm, that She might surge always in the blood tides of our bodies and hearts.

The Gift of Rhythm and Blood

T THE BEGIN-
ning of the beginning, the Goddess Danu glittered tiny as a
fairy in the mists. You'd scarce have seen Her, even had you
been there, for the swirl of milky gray about Her gossamer self.
But Danu was there, sure as we're here: a glistening globe of
possibility at the start of it all.

It was Danu's dreamtime then. Asleep, Her thoughts quiv-
ered and swelled. Awake, She held Her face in Her hands,
wondering and humming, lost in Her own stillness. It may well
have been the dreams that caused the growing. The dreams
trickled at first and then flooded in the pearly dark place between sleeping and waking, where time is like water and nothing is impossible. But whether it came from the dreaming or
something else, Danu the Goddess grew. Oh, it surprised Her
how She grew!

It was Her legs at first. She extended them to relieve their aching and splayed Her toes. Somehow those spread toes came to hold whole bays between their peninsular lengths, and Her limbs stretched lopingly long. Hard and round and luscious they'd become—with knees and thighs fair like mountains, they were so huge. Her arms shot from their sockets and came to end in gigantic slender-fingered hands in which She could suddenly see the streams and creeks of veins. The once plump little wrists took on the definition of hills—and, oh! the down of Her fore-arms resembled meadows more than anything. Her neck, too, had lost its cushion and got a swivel to match the capacity of Her stride.

How shy this Danu, how astounded! How full of Her change She was, once wee as an idea and now enormous as the world. She had flitted once, effortlessly. Now Her movements felt tremendous and heavy. Danu mused, twirling absently a tuft of hair behind Her ear. Then She heaved Herself into the sleep of exhaustion, only to wake to even more growing.

Danu opened Her eyes to the sight of dark green sprouts on the soft triangle below Her navel. Gingerly, She fingered these spiky curling firs and then delighted Herself when they didn't fall away. More sprang up, in the valleys under Her arms and on the lush three-sided range between Her legs, until those sweet places were most forested with trees.

And then, before She slept again, Danu's breasts grew. Gone were the days when She could arch Her chest and de-scribe a smooth bridge between belly and neck! Now that arch was soft and spilling as twin mountains tipped by ranunculi and grazed by sheep! Danu touched a ranunculus and bit Her lower lip in Her teeth.

When Danu plunged again into sleep, She dreamed this time of a great ball of fire in the sky that splintered the mists around Her as the music of a pipe and drum fill a silence. When She awoke, Her haunches felt sure and deep and She found a river of blood flowing between Her legs. Danu tasted the rosy wetness in wonder and turned Her eyes to the sky. Immediately

She was sugared with a yellow warmth, and the skin of Her shoulders expanded with pleasure.

"You're My dream!" She cried out, and Her eyes glinted in the light.

"I'm Your dream," a voice agreed. "I am Dagdu the Sun."

Danu cast down Her eyes, and Her smile dazzled when She turned them up again. "Do stay, Dagdu the Sun," said Danu the Earth. "I can't tell You how good You feel!"

"Oh, I will stay, lovely green, brown, and red Lady!" said the voice. "I will stay."

Danu sighed and turned over. Dagdu the Sun broke all the way through the mists and beat down on the body of the Goddess. She fell asleep there in the heat. Who knows how long She slept, but when She awoke this time, Dagdu was gone. Danu sat up and caught up the back of Her hair in Her hand. She looked at the silvery clouds and remembered Dagdu's delicious warmth. Then She looked down and put Her hand on the place where the river of blood had come. How soft and good it felt there! The wetness lay in a pool beside Her, but it had ceased to flow. She moved Her hand up to the wings of Her pelvis and then dipped them again to the cave between Her legs. For surely that's what She felt: a deep, wet cavern that nestled in the protection of the two mountains of Her bones.

How pleased Danu was to see Her Dagdu again! For in His absence, She'd begun to think of Him that way—as Her Dagdu, Her wonderful Sun whose light would shine especially for Her delight. Not far from the truth, either, that way of thinking, for it happened that Dagdu Himself came to think never so clearly as when He imagined His Danu and felt never so free as when He held Her in His arms. For that's what became of the friendship of Earth and Sun. They talked to each other; they traced each other's noses and bit each other's palms. They made each other shout with laughter. One day Danu told Dagdu about the dark, secret place under Her forests. Dagdu's voice was tender when He asked if He could look inside.

It was Dagdu who told Her about the smooth, round globe at the back of Her cave that changed again and again from pale

51

mauve to the color of wine. For Danu did finally invite Dagdu to flood Her dark with His light, and it was once in a reverie that followed a time when They had held each other in this way that Danu had Her dream of making animals and people. She awoke flushed and intense with excitement. Dagdu kissed the ridge of Her cheek when She told Him and plucked away the damp tendril of hair that clung to Her forehead. "It's a wonderful dream," He said.

On the evening of the day Danu followed Her dream and formed animals and people of the soft Earth of Her breasts and the pool of blood beside Her, Dagdu told Her that She'd never looked so beautiful. "When You pursed Your lips up like that and set the people moving with Your breath! Hmmmm! The scent of You, Danu! You are amazing," He said, and nestled His head in Her neck. The sky grew soft and pink around that comely couple while They watched the animals mew and burrow for cover and the humans sing tunes and smear their mouths purple with currants.

Perhaps an eon passed before Danu and Dagdu had the argument. Couples will argue, you know, much as they may also please each other, for they are not one but two beings and so they are bound to see and feel things differently. But isn't it true that the argument that makes one so cross at the time can, not so much later, be the inspiration for wonderful change? It was certainly that way with the argument of Danu and Dagdu, for out of Their misunderstanding came the very rhythm of our world.

Danu had been dreaming again, asleep in Dagdu's embrace. She jerked awake suddenly one night, shaking with the cracked pieces of a nightmare inside Her.

"Dagdu!" Danu's voice was sharp.

"Hmmmm." Dagdu's voice was dim with sleep.

"Dagdu. I dreamed that My people forget Me." The God heard the pellets of fear in Danu's voice. He lay His finger on Her lips and made hushing noises while He rocked Her against Him.

Danu may have returned to sleep, but She spoke urgently again about the dream in the morning. Dagdu was languid and toyed with Her little finger as She talked. "What was it, darling?" He said.

Danu couldn't remember the images. She just knew it was a terrible feeling of dread She had and this knowing that Her people had forgotten Her.

"Darling, they're not going to forget You!" Dagdu said soothingly. "You *made* them, honey. They can't forget."

"I can't explain it," said Danu. "But it was as if the people—I think there were thousands of them—as if they thought I were dead, but I was really alive. It was horrible." Danu turned Her head away.

Dagdu curled four of Her fingers around one of His own. "Danu, they can't forget either of Us," He said. His voice was teasing. "They certainly can't forget *Me*, anyway. I'm much too hot and warm, and I feel too good."

Danu snatched Her hand away. Now Dagdu had meant, I'm sure, to nuzzle Her with His teasing and relax Her with His caresses. However, Dagdu had the handicap of not having dreamed Danu's dream, and Danu's averted head prevented Her from seeing the playful sympathy on Dagdu's face. She heard only the lightness of His mood in contrast to Her own despair, and She was furious.

A black wind came up and the Goddess stayed alone for a long time. She wept and She slept. She screamed and She dreamed. She felt the curve and the flatness of Herself. She watched Her blood river come and go. She spoke aloud and unraveled the meaning and horror of that nightmare about a kind of aloneness not healing and full of truth like this one, but dangerous and a lie.

Slowly there grew in Danu a plan, details blurred at first. But came the day when it was clear and simple as if She'd known it all along.

First She reached inside the cave of Herself and drew out the globe that Dagdu had told Her waxed and waned with a cycle He said seemed to match Her desire to lie in His arms.

53

She gazed at it creamy and gray in Her palm and remembered the uninterrupted mists of Her beginnings. Then She hung it in the sky and called it Moon.

Next Danu called to Her all the people that had breasts and valleys like Her own. Like Herself, She told them, they would bleed, in rhythm with Her Moon, rivers between their legs so that they and those who love them might ever remember Her. Like Herself, they would find refuge and joy in both the light and the dark.

The people were thrilled with Danu's plan. In their village, they made a temple like Danu's cave with long narrow windows to welcome Dagdu's light. They drew on the walls there the story of the ebb and flow of the blood river by counting its days with careful marks. They pecked its clock with circular spirals on giant stones. They painted red the door of Her sacred triangle to mark the place from which all had come and to which they would return.

Danu, too, was filled with peace. Maybe you can imagine that speechless shyness with which She reopened Her friendship with Dagdu. How the words tumbled when the shyness melted. And how much They had to tell about what each had learned in the time of solitude and introspection. Time passed and They repeated the cycle again and again. It was true, They agreed. Never did They feel so verdant, so radiant, as when They came together again after the renewal of separation.

And so it was with Danu's humans. Never did the world throb so rightly as when the people remembered to sing in the cave of their Goddess and to dance in the light of their God. Ever through time has circled this remembering, even in the days when the people, as Danu once dreamed, are so close to forgetting Her. But Her wonderful plan, born in the contemplation of Her terror, prevents forgetting. For in the bodies of Danu's women flows Her river, and in Her sky moves Her Moon. And so for women, and all those who love them, the Goddess lives. Tiny as a fairy in the mists, perhaps, or gigantic as the world. She lives.

Kali (KAH-lee)
Dancer on Gravestones
(India)

Introduction

Although most commonly understood in Her Destroyer aspect, the Goddess Kali is the full Triple Goddess of the Hindu religion. She is the Ocean of Menstrual Blood at the Beginning of Time, out of whose nourishment comes all life. She is the Mother Fountain of Endless Love, and, in the same way that the monthly blood shedding of a human woman destroys the possibility of life for a cycle, She is the Ender of All. She is the hungry Earth, who devours Her own children.

Like Maya, Devi, and Shakti (see stories), Kali is the Primordial Feminine, out of Whom all comes and to Whom all returns. It is in Her Destroyer aspect, however, that She most upsets the colloquial image of the Goddess in the West. Her squatting, many-armed form, with Her bared teeth and necklace of skulls, with the corpse of Her consort Shiva beneath Her, defies once and for all our stereotype of the Goddess as a combination of a nymph, Cleopatra, and Florence Nightingale.

55

In relationship to the Corpse God Shiva, Kali is the aspect of the Goddess Shakti that precedes and follows another revival of Shiva as Lord of the Dance: She is the Goddess alone in the majesty of Her totality. For the God Shiva, along with His masculine counterparts, Brahma and Vishnu, is like the water contained in the hollow made by a cow's hoof compared with the vast sea of Their Goddess.

To write the story of Kali, I took my notebook and pen on a walk in Oakland's Redwood Park. I had spent the evening before calling Her name and asking for help. I wanted to portray death and the human relationship to death in a way that captured neopaganism's diametric opposition to the Christian concept of death as punishment for sin. I left the trail to sit cross-legged under deep shade in piles of evergreen needles. I chewed the pen and whispered Her name. The draft story came, and, with a sense of peace and accomplishment, I arose in a couple of hours to return home. I found my clothes covered with tiny white maggots. The moment was perfect: Kali was there.

Kali's colors are red, black, and white. She can be invoked with a knife, skull, or cauldron.

The Story of Death

HERE IS NOT enough room!" the people were crying. "There is not enough room!"

It was true. Plants were so thick on the forest floors that the strongest knives could not cut paths through them. Corn and rice grew so high in the fields that they towered like trees over the people. People had not enough to eat in those times, because no one died. Babies came and grew bigger and bigger, but people did not get old and they never left the Earth.

That was when the Goddess Kali turned over in Her sleep. The peoples' cry, "There's not enough room!" became part of Her dream. But She must have been ready to awake because the next cry, "There's not enough room!" woke Her and She sat up. "You disturb My sleep!" She bellowed, rubbing Her eyes with Her fists.

"There's not enough room!" the people cried.

Kali drew on Her robes. She walked to Her window and threw it open to look out on the world. She put Her dark hands on the sill and leaned out. Her black hair ruffled in the wind. What She saw made Her draw back into Her room.

She saw crowds of people piled on each other, none of them old, all of them elbowing each other to get at vats of food in buildings crammed together so tightly it was hard to see the sky. Animals swarmed through the throngs. The air was hot with sweat and perfume and soil.

Kali, inside, licked Her lips. Her hands went to Her hips. "Time!" She yelled.

Her servant, Time, came running. "Bring Me My red sari," She ordered. Time brought the garment, dark as the color of blood.

Kali threw off the gray robes of sleep and fastened the red about Her. "Clothe yourself," She said to Her servant. "We are going out. And bring Me My jewels."

Time did as bidden. He took up Her gray robes for himself and put on shoes the shape of fish. Then he brought Kali Her necklace, glinting with skulls.

"Take these," Kali said, and She thrust gifts wrapped in golden paper into Time's hands. "Now call My chariot!"

The chariot came, pulled by eight white stallions and eight black mares. Fire leapt from its wheels when Kali and Time climbed to its platform. With a loud cry, Kali raised Her hand and let loose the rein.

The horses smoked across the distance to Earth. Before each village, Kali drew in the rein. Her servant Time stepped from the chariot and handed the gold-wrapped gifts to people who crowded at each stop.

In each package the people found Kali's gifts. Spider webs. Dust. Decay. Mold. Worms. Rust. Mushrooms. Crumbling. Rot. Mildew. The smell of rich earth. Aging.

It was on that day that crops knew more than just blooming and growing. They knew also the withering that returned them to the soil. It was on that day that the plants of the forest floor began to add to the blackness of the soil so the trees could grow.

58

Animals had babies, but now the babies grew old. Humans too began to age. They also began to die, so there would be room for their children.

Kali and Her servant Time returned to Her palace. Exhausted She fell, still crimson-clothed, across Her bed. Time undressed Her gently and tucked Her under the covers.

Kali is the Goddess who dances at funerals and sometimes stops babies from being born. Kali still rides with Her servant, Time. Since that first trip, though, Time has carried his own presents. Time gives people the gift of white hairs, and he wraps them carefully in the gold paper of wisdom and acceptance.

Changing Woman

(Navajo People)

Introduction

The Navajo People of southwest North America think of the processes of Nature as Woman. Estsan Atlehi, Woman Changing, they call Her. In the person of Changing Woman, the Navajo anthropomorphize Nature and remind us, in turn, that the tick of our human natures resembles none other than Earth's endless fluctuations. The Navajo people see Her, as do the Arunta people of Australia (see story of Sun Woman), as able to metamorphose, endlessly, becoming both young and old again and again.

Embedded in the wisdom of Changing Woman is also the truth that She cannot be defied. To the people who taught us this way of seeing Earth, Euroamericans owe a great debt they are just beginning to realize. For despite vast differences in language and social structure, the peoples we today call Native Americans, who migrated to North America at least twelve thousand years ago, revere the living world. They use night

60

dreams as sources of wisdom and respect plants and animals as teaching spirits. Their tradition can show us the ways of walking lightly on the Trail of Beauty called life on Earth.

Changing Woman's story is a retelling of Her traditional myth as related by Merlin Stone in *Ancient Mirrors of Womanhood*. Changing Woman's power and comfort is the unrelenting constancy of Her shifts. I have invoked Her by placing a ring or hoop on my altar. Sweeping and mundane, Her presence works in my life. I have tried to convey Her dependable as a bathrobe wrapped around me while the hotcakes steam.

Between Things That Are Different

AS THE QUES-
tion Why? ever split you like a bent fork and left you shiny and
pointed with pain? Perhaps the phone rang then or the laundry
needed drying, and the pulse of the world pushed the why
behind you.

Has the why returned later, but this time flat and quiet, still
with you, but not twisted in the same way now?

There is a very small pocket of time between the sharp
question and the event that makes you forget. Into that small
pocket of time the Goddess Changing Woman flies. Changing
Woman flies in, and She fills up the pocket.

Changing Woman comes to stay in spaces of time between
things that are different. She is there between the clock-time start
of the weekend and the body-time start. She is there between
the time you choose your trip's destination and the moment the
seat belt fastens about you for your journey home. Changing
Woman fills up the time after the fitful, sobbing nights and
before your cactus soul bursts into pink blossom again.

Changing Woman is hard to see. The pockets of time She lives in are small and fleeting, and She is always moving. Sometimes She's beside you, sometimes She's underneath you, and sometimes She's inside your heart. Sometimes She's in yesterday, and sometimes She's a few minutes from now. Sometimes She is Girl, other times Teenager. Sometimes She's big and strong. Other times Her hair is snow white and She walks with a turquoise cane.

Changing Woman lay kicking and gurgling at the beginning of the world. In the pocket of time at the beginning, before the mountains heaved themselves out of the mist, Baby Changing Woman laughed and clapped Her hands in a basket of red flowers. When the mountains humped up high, Baby Changing Woman shouted and changed from Baby to Child. She climbed out of Her basket and the winds came to play with Her, then the rains. Child Changing Woman sang, and grasses blew in the valleys. Trees popped from the hills.

In the pocket of time before the Sun came out, Changing Woman turned into Girl. She kicked over the basket of red flowers and scattered the petals. Everywhere a petal landed, an animal grew. The petals on the land became beaver, buffalo, squirrel, and grasshopper. The petals on the breeze grew into birds. The petals in the water dove into fish.

While the animals turned into parents of eggs and fluff, Changing Woman became Woman and walked a Trail of Beauty in the World. She turned Her neck this way and that. "I see Ten Thousand Things," said Woman Changing Woman. "They are beautiful and I am glad."

Changing Woman grew hungry in the next pocket of time. She killed a buffalo and cooked the soft red meat for Her meal. She made a brown bed of buffalo's fur. She slept on Her buffalo bed for many nights and days.

Changing Woman soaked Herself in a side pool of the sunlit river when She awoke. In the pocket of time between scrubbing and rubbing Her dark skin with buffalo's fat, She turned into Mother. Men and women slipped from between Mother Changing Woman's thighs. Children sprang from Her belly. Mother Changing Woman turned Her neck back and forth and watched Her people build homes and make families.

Changing Woman's skin wrinkled while She watched. Wrinkled Changing Woman taught the people how to plant kernels of corn, how to pick the sweet yellow ears, and how to grind the dried corn into meal for cooking. Wrinkled Changing Woman gave the people songs for being born, songs for growing up, and other songs for dying. Wrinkled Changing Woman gave the Earth the Time of Hot and the Time of Cold. When the people see Changing Woman in the Time of Hot, they call Her Mother and say Her muscles are hard while She pounds the laundry white at the edge of the river. When they see Her in the Time of Cold, they call Her Grandmother and say She looks thin and frail as She walks oh so slowly across the snow.

People come to Changing Woman for many things. "Teach us to weave, Changing Woman. Teach us to gallop," the people beg. And in the time between the tangled skeins and the blanket, in the time between the clumsiness of two and the ripple of one running, Changing Woman is at work.

"Changing Woman, why did my dog die?" asks a girl. And between the death and the funeral she holds by planting a seed where she buries the dog, Changing Woman is there. Changing Woman lives in the time before the new dog comes. She is present when the seed sprouts into a bush. And She is there when the new dog and the girl grow older together.

"Changing Woman, what is this life about?" ask a man and a woman. "We don't understand." That's when Changing Woman looks like Girl. Only Her teeth show that She is Old. When She smiles, they are full of gold.

"Come with Me," beckons Changing Woman to the woman and the man, giving each a red flower. "Come walk with Me on the Trail of Beauty." In the pocket of time between the asking and the asking again, the woman and man walk with Changing Woman. On the Trail of Beauty with Changing Woman, the people walk. On the Trail of Beauty, the people see, hear, feel, taste, and smell all of the Ten Thousand Things.

Isis (EYE-sis)
Queen of the World
(Egypt)

Introduction

Like Freya of Scandinavia and Juno of Rome (see stories), Isis is the Greek name for the Egyptian Goddess of the Thousand Names in the Completeness of Her Majesty. Queen of Healing and Magic, Mistress of the Gods, Isis of Egypt was actively worshiped for three and a half thousand years, nearly twice as long as Christ. Pyramid texts of 3000 B.C.E. refer to the "Great Isis," and the final suppression of Her official worship came not until 426 C.E., a century after Constantine had declared Christianity the acceptable religion of the Roman Empire. Her geographical range was enormous: when Alexander the Great conquered Egypt in 332 B.C.E., he began to spread the word of the Mother of Life from emperors' palaces to private homes and marketplaces, until finally Her honor reached from Egypt to the River Thames in London.

Called Au Set by the Egyptians, Isis, Separator of Heaven and Earth and Inventor of Agriculture, sheltered the pharaohs in Her winged lap. In the myth that recapitulates the death and resurrection of the annual vegetation cycle, Isis is Sister-Wife-Mother to Horus-Osiris, the male God who dies as a seed is buried in order to return again to life with the flood of Her water. (See stories of Inanna and Ereshkigal, and Demeter and Persephone.) Indeed, the overflow of the Nile is said to be Her tears of agony as Isis searches with Her Sister Nephthys of the Underworld for the pieces of Her Osiris, killed and mutilated in a rage by Set, the God of Destruction. The Sister Goddesses re-member Osiris, and Isis, pregnant by the revivified God, gives birth to Son Horus, who is His Father's reborn self.

Isis, the Compassionate One, She Who has suffered, also reigns over all that is miraculous, even as the endless cycle of the harvest never ceases to bless and astonish. Present at child-birth and guide on death's journey, Isis satisfied humanity through Her humanness, and Her realm came to include even the sea as people of many languages and locations clasped Her to their hearts. Isis is the Black Madonna of today's eastern Europe and, with Her Son Horus, the prototype of all Christian Madonna-Child images.

I use feathers to remind me of the winged arms of Isis, which represent to me Her power to comfort, protect, and to soar in healing and transformation. I wrote Her story to invoke the intense personal humanity of Her presence.

The Story of Life

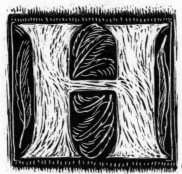

ORUS-OSIRIS THE
Land sat in the lap of His Mother, Isis, the River. Cuddled
there in Her great winged arms, Horus-Osiris heard the story
of life. Isis told Osiris about the stars and about the wind. She
told Him about wisdom and healing. She told Him of turquoise
and sailboats and the sticky brown date fruit in the desert.

"And Me, Mama?" asked Osiris. "Tell a story about Me."

"You, Osiris," said Isis, "are the keeper of all the plants and
seeds of the world."

"Like the barley and wheat?" asked Osiris.

"Like the barley and wheat," said Isis. "Like the little barley
and little wheat that must cuddle in the dark 'til they grow big
enough for people to pick and eat."

"I am little now," said Osiris. "Am I like a barley seed?"

"Yes, just like a barley seed," said Isis.

"Mama, will I get big like the barley and wheat?" asked Osiris.

"You will get big, My Son," said Isis.

"Will the people pick Me?"

"The people will pick You."

"But Mama, I will be in pieces then! And if people eat Me up, where will the new little barleys and wheats come from?"

Isis hugged Osiris very close. She kissed Him many times on the top of His head. Horus-Osiris wiggled to look at Isis. "Mama! Why are You crying?"

"I am crying, Osiris, because You will grow big and You will go away from Me. The people will pick You, and You will be in pieces. And I will miss You. . . . But . . ."

"Mama! I don't want to go away from You!" Osiris wrapped His arms tight around His Mother's neck.

"But, Osiris, I will pick a piece of You, too. And I will swallow You down to My lap again—just like We are now."

Osiris pulled away from Isis and looked for a long time at Her face. Then with His fingers, He petted the soft feathers of Her wings.

"Mama, will I get big like that soon?"

Isis sighed. "Soon enough, Son," She said.

"Mama," said Osiris, "If I get big, then little on Your lap, will I get big again?"

"Yes," said Isis.

"And then little, and big, then little—over and over?" asked Osiris.

"Over and over," said Isis.

"Will You always remember to swallow me when I'm in pieces?" asked Osiris.

"Always," said Isis. "I will never forget."

"Mama," said Osiris, "Is that because We're magic?"

"Yes, My Son," said Isis. "It's because We're magic."

"Good night, Mama," said Horus-Osiris, and He put two fingers in His mouth.

"Good night, Osiris," said Isis, and She folded Her wings over Her Son to shut out the light.

The Three Zoryas (ZOR-yahs)
Keepers of Dawn, Day, and Night
(Russia)

Introduction

The Zoryas are Goddesses whose mythology is rooted in the northern Slavic land of the primeval forests. In Russia, for example, the forest is the nursery of culture, and its beauty and danger color customs and stories. Food and friendship are hard to find in that cold, dense land, and its peoples compensated by developing warm traditions of hospitality. Life in the frozen forest was built around the dwelling in the clearing and its source of heat. Indeed, heat, not light, is the way to the spirit.

Slavic peoples in these regions dealt with harsh seasonal cycles; the ebb and flow of nomadic conquerors; the constant possibility of fires gone out of control; and insects and rodents gnawing up from below. In this beautiful but unfriendly context was born the Triple Goddess known as the Three Zoryas or the Dawn Goddess (Zorya Utrennyaya); the Morning Star Goddess (Zvezda Dennitsa); and the Sunset or Evening Star

Goddess (Zorya Vechernyaya). The myth of the Three Zoryas gives Them responsibility for keeping the Dog of Destruction tied securely to the constellation Ursa Minor, lest it run loose and end the world.

The ancient religions of the Slavs respected natural processes: the ripening as fruit ripens and the growing as grass grows. They kept alive a passion for seeing beauty and spiritual truth in concrete rather than abstract forms.

While writing the story of the Three Zoryas, I felt as if I were painting instead, so tangible did I feel their loving, steadfast, absolute warmth to be. Sometimes I make tea and do housework, very slowly, in honor of the Zoryas. And because, to me, They are the Great Boundary Keepers, I use a piece of rope on my altar to symbolize the strength and flexibility of Their help with interpersonal boundaries between myself and other people.

The House of Heat for the Beloved Visitor

A T THE TOP OF the forest that reaches the heavens live the Three Zoryas, who endlessly tend the dawn, the day, and the night. Safe from the fighting, the frosts, and the fires live the Three Zoryas in a dark wooden hut next to the corral of the Sun. Ever heating in that hut is the stove on which swells hot bread and steams the samovar for tea for the beloved visitor.

"Stay! Stay!" welcome the Zoryas, bundling the traveler's blue hands and wet feet in furs. They give her the place of honor right next to the glowing heat.

Over and over again the Zoryas renew her tea; they light a beeswax candle and make ready for her a bed of piney boughs. No matter the length of time that passes here in this fragrant home, the visitor is warm and fed; always she is safe from the fighting, the frost, and the fires.

And no matter the length of time that passes here, always Grandmother Zorya is first up at the dawn. White haired and slow moving, She kindles again the stove. No matter the pain She might have in the joints of Her hips that morning, Grandmother Zorya leaves the hut at the break of light for the corral of the Sun Horses.

She croons softly to them as She unlatches the ancient gate. They are nickering and nibbling at their troughs, and their faces are beautiful and aware as Grandmother Zorya's wrinkled hand lets swing the gate. The colder the air, the slower She moves, but finally, never failing, She opens the gate. Like the burst of energy from a hot popping log, the white horses break and snort and plunge rippling and smooth into the sky with the light of the Sun expanding pink and aqua about them. Grandmother Zorya returns then to the hut, where She sets the samovar again to boil.

Early or late the Sun Horses may have begun their gallop, but always the Maiden Zorya makes Her way too into the day. When the visitor follows and climbs the hill behind the hut, she may see the Maiden Zorya setting out against the immaculate liquid blue of the sky. Or, on a day when the air is cold, Maiden Zorya moves quickly, and sometimes the visitor can barely discern Her thick bundled form against the clouds. The winds then drown any sound of the Sun Horses' hooves and the visitor returns early to the warmth of the hearth.

But on a day when the hooves still echo to the listener on the hill, Maiden Zorya is a dream of muscle and laughter in the field below the stable flung wide, where even the new fallen dung smells of the fresh air. There that sturdy Maiden Zorya tosses the heavy yield of the hay while the poppies seethe in the open space and the birds grow fat on wild berries. If She disappears, perhaps She is gathering mushrooms, moss, or bark deep in the forest. But always She returns in the soft or the swelter: the moss will cover the floor of the hut, the bark will make shoes and paper. The thoughts of the visitor might whisper on this day. Or, for the colors alone she might break into song. Sometimes the visitor might nap with her Maiden Zorya, right there on the billow of the green hill while the plums on the tree overhead purple in the light.

No matter whether the time is passed hunting in cool green leaf of forest, or reaping in the yellow ocean of rye, always the strength of the Maiden Zorya spends itself finally and She and Her visitor walk arm in arm back to their supper.

The birch trees at the edge of the corral are dappled and their leaves take on the sheen of fading light. Mother Zorya, Keeper of the Night, covers Her head against the deepening chill and walks slowly to the gate of the corral. She readies the water and the hay for the tired animals. Closer and closer trot the Sun Horses. The sunlight behind them is like a cut melon, delicious and cold in the paling sky. Whinnying greeting, flanked in sweat, the Sun Horses fill the corral with their aliveness and Mother Zorya shuts firm the gate. Perhaps She stays inside the corral to brush the coats of the animals. Perhaps She just sits, still and silent, watching the quiet animals sink their noses to their feed. The light is dove colored now; shadows melt and mingle, colors mute. The visitor inside the hut feels a longing and a sadness in her chest.

Mother Zorya must do another task before Her never-failing work is through. The horses are fed and watered; the gate is shut tight. Now She must feed the dog chained to the iron stake at the sky place where the stars take the form of the Little Bear.

The visitor is wistful. She wishes Mother Zorya would hurry with Her errand. She will feel complete and able to drop away to sleep only when all Three Zoryas sit together by the crackling hearth. She offers to help Mother Zorya carry the bucket of scraps to the dog in the sky.

Together they travel. The darkness is gleaming now with stars. The visitor feels afraid when She sees the dog. The dog is thin. It strains at the chain, teeth bared, hairs high on its neck, ears back. Mother Zorya calls softly. The visitor hangs back and watches. Mother Zorya heaves the contents of the pail before the dog. The animal tenses. But its ears are forward now and its eyes are sad. Mother Zorya talks gently. The dog throws itself to its meal.

73

"No matter how much it eats, it is hungry," says Mother Zorya. "It is the Dog of Agony and Destruction. It is always afraid, but I always come. I never forget."

The dog seems sated now. It is lying down. Only its hindquarters are tensed. The visitor feels a lump in her throat.

She returns with Mother Zorya to the hut, empty bucket wobbling between them.

Embers glow, sinking to ashes. The Zoryas—Grandmother, Maiden, Mother—sing the visitor to sleep. The Sun Horses stand, leaning their big heads on one another in the dark.

That visitor might be you. The Zoryas make you welcome any time. They are delighted to see you. There in Their hut, safe from the fighting, the frosts, and the fires, you may sip the tea of Their cheerful little samovar. It is there you may repair when you need to firmly shut the gate of your corral, to say no, this is done, this is enough. It's time to eat and be inside. Or it is there you may go when it's time to open your gate, to let the flood of your expression and strength prance, wind playing in the fine hair of your mane. Or perhaps you will linger there, because timidity and hopelessness fill you. Perhaps then you will remember to feed the dog who strains at your chain, whose eyes turn from wild to lonely and whose fears you may quiet for a time with your devoted attention. Perhaps you will visit that hut of the Zoryas because They are the Limit Setters, the Boundary Keepers, and you need Their unflagging responsiveness to the slow rhythm of your day. Maybe you will come when it's hard to say yes. Then Grandmother Zorya and Maiden Zorya will help you fling your gate and fill your sky. Maybe you will come when you are terrified to say no and the unknown snarls before you like the fangs of a beast. Then Mother Zorya will help you shut your gate and feed the endless questions until the morning comes.

III

Spirit Incarnate:
Goddess As Earth and Body

In Mexico, I was struck by the slang word *carnal* (accent on the last syllable) used by men to call a buddy something equivalent to "brother" or "bro." It seemed a wonderful word to me: the word *carnal* in the fundamentalist Christianity of my youth had always been spoken in the same breath as *sin*. In phrases that never failed to intrigue me, ministers would explain that we Christians were not to be "of this earth, earthy," and that we were to "put away the things of this world."

My body, in the religion of my childhood, was a trap. Though we called it a "temple," I was taught that it would betray me and lead me astray from the "paths of righteousness." Because, like most children, I was interested in feats of prowess, conquering my body and its desires appealed to me. Especially in settings in which grownups were unable to acknowledge, let alone meet, my needs, why not just get rid of needs? Why not accept a philosophy that made desire and sensation the lowest of the low on a hierarchy that conceived of even the word *base* as bad?

Living in my head made a lot of sense in a context in which physical and emotional feelings appropriate to circumstance were not allowed. Sensation would just get me into trouble, I reasoned. My religious teachers must be right. Better I should make my highest concern control of my body and feelings.

Such a mind-set was abetted, of course, by the larger, secular culture. Just as the religious culture equated the color black with sin, the secular culture associated black with bad, dirty, and ugly. The religious culture admonished control of the body; the secular culture pressed the same restrictions, particularly on people labeled as more "physical" than "mental": children, women, and people of color. Ferret out what needs fixing and adjust it. Tone it down, keep it together, sit up straight, be quiet, and keep a smile on your face. Erase yourself.

Earth, in the culture of control, is a list of resources that need to be managed. Like women, children, and people of color, Earth, in control culture, should look nice but cause no trouble. Across history and in the present time, peoples who do not have controlling relationships with Earth tend to identify with the Earth. They see the Earth as live and animate; they relate to the spirits in rocks, foxes, and rivers. Throughout the history of control culture, the stories of people identified with Earth have been crushed, their images misshapen, and their lands taken for "resource value." Like the minds and bodies of girls, women, and people of color, the Earth Herself has been stripped, raped, poisoned, desecrated, and left for dead.

But like the people who are Her consciousness, the Earth has begun to rise again. Over and over again I hear the stories of people, otherwise steeped in rational, left-brain thinking, who feel they hear the call of the Great Feminine Flow of Life, asking them to stand and create for Her. Left for dead She has been, but She has not died. Like a part of ourselves crushed or swollen, shaking with effort, She is reviving Herself. She is calling racism, sexism, classism, ageism, homophobia, and colonialism by the name of body hatred, and She is linking the politics of control back to the abuse of Herself. She is making us wonder how our personal insistence on consumer convenience is really different from the sense of entitlement with which the corporate colonizer turns a forest into a beef ranch. She is promising us that feelings count: the agony and the anger teach us where we are. She is assuring us that our desires help us clean our house: pretending we have no needs is a recipe for victimization.

The Goddess is Earth. She is incarnate. She is knowing, willing, daring, and silence. She is East, South, West, and North. Out of Her silent North body coils East's knowing. Out of the knowing blazes South's will. Out of South's fire floods West's daring waters of change. North's body accepts the imprint of Her change. In silence comes again East's mindfulness that bends South's will and frees West's daring. And so on for us everlasting.

Freya (FRAY-uh)
Mother of All
(Scandinavia)

Introduction

L ike Au Set of Egypt, called Isis by the Greeks, and Juno of Rome (see stories), Freya was the northern European Goddess whose totality of power was worshiped by Her peoples, even when they called Her by a hundred different names. Widely revered by country people for centuries after states had claimed Christianity as the official religion, She was a reality with which Catholic authorities in Germany, Scandinavia, and Iceland had to reckon. Recognizing that prohibiting Her honor altogether was impossible, the church both co-opted and diabolized Her symbols. Thus, for example, they taught that Friday, Freya's sacred day, was really a Catholic holy day on which fish, one of Her sacred animals, was to be eaten. And they plunged Her magical number thirteen into disrepute. Luckiest of lucky, Freya's thirteen, the number of the moon and menstrual cycles in a year, became the number to be shunned, especially when it fell on Friday, which would have doubled its power for Her worshipers.

Like other forms of the Great Goddess, Freya was identified with the land itself. She was thus the embodiment of sexual love, tenderness, beauty, and nurture, as well as the mud of the Underworld, the tomb of all living. The Sow, known for Her tremendous fertility; the usefulness of all Her parts to humans; and Her ability to compost even Her own feces inside Herself, was another of Freya's symbols. Her priestesses, women known as the Volva, functioned as both oracular wise women and judges of Her principles of right living, justice, honor, and peace.

Freya's story is my variation of one found in the thirteenth-century C.E. *Prose Edda* of Snorri Sturluson. I turn to Freya to overcome my despair about Earth's bondage. I invoke Her with images of the globe, the pig, the black cat, and the number thirteen.

The Story of Who Owns the Land

HE OLD ONES say that Freya, Eartha, Mother of All, Goddess of the Plow, Mistress of Cats, She of the Sacred Thirteen Moons, Goddess of Love, the Great Sow Mother, comes riding on Fridays to dispense Her wisdom to those who seek it and engentle the lives of those weary in body and sick at heart. It is on Fridays that the people eat of Her sacred fish, bathe themselves in perfumed hot waters, and cling to their beloveds with sweet abandon.

Freya comes riding, they say, in Her chariot of light, drawn by thirteen cats as sleek and black as night. Swift and silent She comes, they say, to those who call out Her name for comfort and truth. So quick and noiseless is She, they say, that always some forget Her power and forget to call out Her name.

That is so now, and it was so even a thousand years ago on a Friday night in the dead of winter, under the shining moon.

Two neighbors stood there in the snow shaking their fists and shouting at each other. Friends and relatives bundled in furs circled them, stamping and calling punctuations to their fight.

"This land is mine, fool!" yelled the taller, whose name was Angantyr.

"It's mine, I tell you," said Ottar, the other. He put his face close to Angantyr's and jabbed his finger. "And even if it weren't mine, Angantyr," hissed Ottar, "I'd take it from you!"

"I'll use whatever I please to grow my crops on my land, Ottar," rasped Angantyr.

"No poison!" yelled Ottar.

"No poison! No poison!" The friends of Ottar took up the cry.

The argument had begun three years before when Angantyr began to use poison to kill weeds and insects on the rich black land. Angantyr said poison made his work easier and gave him a bigger crop. Ottar said easier or bigger, he didn't care. He would have no poison in his soil, and he said the poison there leached into his water too. Ottar brought a rabbit he'd found bloated and dead to the house of Angantyr. "See what your poison does, Angantyr? Take your poison and get out," he had ordered.

"You get out, Ottar, if you know what's good for you," Angantyr had responded, slamming his door in Ottar's face. And the two neighbors had bickered and raged at each other until tonight, when they stood, sticks in hand, under the shining moon.

"Wait," said a hoarse voice. The excited folk moved aside to let an old woman make a path to the two angry men. The people recognized her by her voice and her limp as the One the Goddess Speaks Through. They saw that with her she dragged a huge bag that twisted and grunted with a live thing inside.

"Ottar and Angantyr," she wheezed. "Freya shall decide on the question of your land."

The group of neighbors crowded close, and a noise rose up among them when the old woman opened the bag. Out of the opening and onto the snow lumbered a huge Mother Pig swollen with the babies She had inside Her.

"Freya," the old woman whispered. The light from the moon shone down on the white and pink of the Sow's back, and the animal stood perfectly still.

"Freya," whispered the people and stepped a little away. Ottar and Angantyr stood breathing hard, but quiet now. The old woman looked sharply at Ottar and then Angantyr and pulled from her hands the skins that covered them. Slowly the two men knelt in the snow. The old woman set a hand each on the shoulders of the kneeling enemies and looked up at the moon.

"Freya!" her voice quavered in the stillness. Then a shudder passed through her. "The rightful owner of this land knows who has owned this land before him," she said. "The one of you who can name the most names of the owners who came before shall own the land. You shall have until the next full moon." The old woman dropped her hands.

"So be it!" said the people and dispersed into the night.

Angantyr and Ottar spent the next month gathering the names of the owners who had come before them. People buzzed with opinions and conjectures about which of the men would have the longest list. Some said Angantyr was sure to win, as he had the best memory. Others said Ottar should win because he loved the land best. "It's not a matter of love!" said others. "Freya requires the names of the owners who came before. That is all. Whoever has the longest list shall own the land."

So the Saturdays and the Sundays, the Mondays and the Tuesdays, the Wednesdays and the Thursdays, and the Fridays rolled around and away. On the night of the next full moon, the people gathered in a barn at the edge of Ottar and Angantyr's land. When they arrived, they found that the One the Goddess Speaks Through was already there. By the side of a small fire she knelt, next to a mound of hay on which lay the Great Mother Sow. At each of the huge Pig's thirteen teats suckled a tiny white and black piglet. The stillness, filled only with the crackle of the fire and the grunts of the babies, was broken by

83

the tramp and bustle of the people. Only when Ottar and Angantyr came and the old woman rose did the people hush.

"Freya hears you now, Angantyr," said the old woman.

Angantyr puffed out his chest and cleared his throat. "I have searched," he said loudly. "By listening to the elders, by reading the records, and by my own memory, I know the ownership of my land backward for seven generations."

A ripple of approval moved through the friends of Angantyr. Seven generations reached far back into time, and if Angantyr could name those names, surely he would win. Ottar could not possibly name names farther back than seven generations.

In a proud voice, Angantyr recited the names of the owners who'd come before him, calling each one the son of the next. His friends cheered when he was finished.

"Freya will hear you now, Ottar," said the old woman.

Ottar, too, cleared his throat. "There are twenty generations right now on my land," he said. "And each of those generations who owns this land goes backward to the beginning of time."

The people's voices rose. What could he mean? Twenty generations? When Angantyr had had seven? Impossible. Ottar was lying.

"Wait," said the old woman. Then she called for another stick of wood for the fire. "Speak, Ottar," she said. The people silenced themselves.

When Ottar spoke, he did not name the human names of a line of fathers and sons. Instead he named the mold and the mushroom, the worm and the grass, the insect and the herb, the spider and the flower, the bee and the mouse, the mole and the minnow, the turtle and the frog, the snake and the tree, the squirrel and the rabbit, and the fox and the hawk. "They are the owners of the land," said Ottar. "Then and now and forever."

And so it was that Ottar that night won the argument with Angantyr. Never more, while those men lived, did poison for weeds or insects spoil the soil and water of that place.

84

Things were different in older times, the old ones say, and some are sure that such wisdom is never more to be heard from the Great Sow Mother.

But there are those who swear that on a Friday night, especially a Friday of the sacred number thirteen, the wisdom of Freya, the Great Sow Mother, can be had by those who call down Her chariot of light drawn by Her sleek black cats whose eyes wink slow as the stars.

Shekina (shuh-KEE-nuh)
Keeper of Wisdom
(Hebrew People)

Introduction

P eople who are uncovering psychological and spiritual truth experience the power of knowing something in the body—not just in the head or even in the heart. Jewish mystical writings, called the Kabbalah, used the word *daath* for the insight that is true because it is accompanied by great feeling. *Daath* is the knowledge that comes from the union of conscious and unconscious minds, a kind of knowing that is a deeply erotic experience. *Daath* is the word used by Kabbalistic writers to refer to the union of God with His Bride, the Sabbath, or the Shekina. The Zohar, the principal book of the Kabbalah, says, "[On the Sabbath] all is found in one body, complete, for the Matronit clings to the King and is become one body, and this is why blessings are found on that day."

Shekina, meaning Sabbath, is the name for the Feast of the Full Moon, which once celebrated the menstruation of the Great Goddess. Originally honored once a month, Her holiness

86

came to be observed once every quarter moon (once a week). The Friday evening that began Her honor was the night in which the husband of the home made love with his wife, recapitulating the union of the God and Goddess. The following day, Saturday, was devoted to the postcoital reverie of washed perceptions and the leisurely depth of feeling that should not be disturbed by mundane doings or materialism.

Patriarchal influence, however, lessened interest in the power of love between the male and female deities within and outside of humans. Consequently, the Sabbath became more an observance obsessed with the minutiae of the law, and the Shekina, once Goddess of Babylon and then of the Jews, went underground.

Her light still glows, however, in the holiness of passionate love, and the braids of Her hair are suggested in the shape of challah bread. Study of the Torah, said to be Her outer garments, can be symbolized in erotic imagery: like a Bride within Her curtained chamber, the Shekina must be courted with the heart, soul, and entire being of those who would know Her wisdom and joy.

Silver candlesticks, white candles, and challah bread all help me to call the Shekina. I wrote this story from the point of view of the young ascetic in me who is still waking to the peace of her own body. Sections of *The Wise Wound* by Penelope Shuttle and Peter Redgrove were invaluable for my understanding of the Shekina.

The Door to the Soul

NCE A YOUNG man asked himself these questions: Who am I? And how am I connected to all others? He wondered and wandered and asked the questions again and again. He yearned for the answers.

One day he approached a teacher and asked, "Who am I? And how am I connected to all others?" The teacher said, "Study will answer those riddles."

"What must I study?" asked the young man.

"Study the thousand and one books," said the teacher. "It is through your study that you will gain wisdom."

So the young man piled the thousand and one books, some dry bread, and some candles on a cart. Then he took himself in cap and shawl, with paper in his shoes for warmth, to a small house at the edge of a town.

Inside the house, at the desk he sat, day after day, reading the thousand and one books. "Who am I?" he wrote on a paper.

"How am I connected to all others?" he wrote on a second. Outside the trees turned fiery and lost their leaves. Inside, the young man filled page after page with learning from his books. He stopped only to swallow a little of the dry bread and sometimes to renew his candle or to drop his aching shoulders before him on the desk to sleep. The young man's wrists grew thin and his eyes burned. The thousand and one books stacked themselves around him in wobbly towers, and the pages of his writings heaped themselves before him like a fence.

One night a freezing rain beat in a torrent against the walls of the house. The young man pulled his shawl tight about him, but he felt the damp like a knife in his back. His feet were numb. The marks on the page before him began to swim. Suddenly the young man let out a moan and flung the book toward the window. "I don't know!" he yelled. "I DON'T KNOW!"

At that very second the rain outside halted and a howl of wind blew up. It clattered the panes and then, in a rush of power, ripped open the catch of the window. The room was filled with the shock of cold air. The candle blew out, and the papers on the desk spattered apart and lifted like the feathers of some giant white bird.

The young man staggered to the window and wrenched it shut. Then turning slowly and looking across the room, he drew back to see that a small light had formed on the other side of the swinging doors that led to the next room. "How can that be?" said the young man. "There is no one in this house but me."

The young man felt afraid. But the light glowed so softly. After a moment, the young man followed the glow to the other side of the doors. The pale light went on before him. This time he had to part a curtain to enter the next room. Still the glow went forward, and the young man found himself walking through room after room. He had not known the house had so many rooms. Was it possible he'd forgotten them? Had they been here before?

Finally the light drew him to a tightly closed door. He pushed it open, and the light settled on a bed in the small room.

The young man breathed out as he saw the light falter, then flare up, and then turn before his eyes into a beautiful Woman.

The Woman's skin was dark and Her hair curled about Her face. Her garment was like the shadows of leaves. She looked quietly at the young man. The bed on which She sat was covered with quilts the color of shells. The walls seemed soft as clouds.

"Who are you?" asked the young man.

"I am your Soul," said the Woman. "I am the Shekina. Eat and be full."

The Woman turned and lifted to the bed a great tray laden with a feast. The young man felt ravenous. Fruit of every sort filled the tray. He fell to it and ate his fill.

The Shekina handed him a cup of steaming broth. The young man felt the warmth seep into his bones. "Bathe now," said the Shekina.

Around him the young man could feel hot, lapping, washing water. Afterward a towel folded around him held in the sweet heat.

"Now. Come. Sleep," said the Shekina. She helped the young man into the bed.

For six days the young man clung to the Shekina, wrapped now in the deepest sleep, then awake and gazing into Her eyes, and then holding Her completely as he could. And then again drifting into the lovely snow of sleep.

On the seventh day, the Shekina rose up and kissed the young man on his lips. Then Her skin seemed to melt and he could no longer see Her features. She faded again to a glow of light. The young man lay unable to move, his breath caught in his throat.

The young man didn't know how long he slept after that. But the next time he opened his eyes, the sun was shining. He gathered up the pits of the fruits he'd eaten and went outside. There in the soil he planted a garden. At the center of the garden he placed a stone. On the stone he wrote these words: "I am one with all. All is one."

Years passed by. The seeds of the fruits grew into a mighty orchard. The young man was no longer young. Now he was an old man who carried his grandchildren.

Always on the seventh day, the old man lit the candles and whispered the story of the calling of the Soul. "Come, Shekina," he would say to the breeze that flickered the candle flames bright. "Come, Shekina, come. Fill this garden with Your rest."

Kuan Yin (kwan YIN)
Mother of Mercy
(China)

Introduction

Like the European Mother of Gods, whose worship as Mary, Star of the Sea, continues to this day against great institutional and theological odds, the Great Goddess of China survived the Buddhization of Her realm by becoming Kuan Yin, Mother of Mercy. Often associated with the waters of the deep, riding a dolphin or a fish, for example, Kuan Yin probably originated in the ancient Nu Kua, the Great Ocean-Snail Snake Dragon Woman who gave birth to all life and the patterns of the universe.

When Buddhism developed about 560 B.C.E., worship of the Mother was already very old. Writers in 2000 B.C.E. exhorted readers to pray to the Grandmother in a land already roamed by humans for a nearly unimaginable 496,000 years. While we do not know how many generations of people in those years revered the Great Feminine, we are almost certain that they recognized only their biological mothers, not their fathers. In such a setting, it is easy to imagine widespread awe for the Female origins of life.

Buddhist storytellers, like their Greek counterparts who told of the Goddess Athena's (see story) paternal birth, said that Kuan Yin was actually a male who had reached a state of Buddha being and then decided to come to Earth as a spiritual teacher in the form of a woman. By masculinizing Her origins, Eastern and Western tellers were undoubtedly trying to grapple with the reality of the Great Feminine in a patriarchal context.

Kuan means Earth, and Yin is the Feminine balance to yang, both of which exist at the root of all the beings and workings of the world. Yin is a state and an energy that flows, creating gentle, consistent, and determined action.

Like Iamanja of Brazil (see story) and the Virgin Mary, Kuan Yin protects, relieves, and comforts in sorrow. She is related to the Japanese Kwannon, still worshiped in the Asakusa district of Tokyo. Her story is a retelling of the traditional one in Merlin Stone's *Ancient Mirrors of Womanhood*.

Because Kuan Yin is as widely worshiped as the Virgin Mary, Her statue is easy to find. She, like Mary, can be called on for healing and mercy and can also be invoked by a willow branch or a white flower floating in a bowl of water.

In the Land of the Dead

HE GODDESS
Kuan Yin longed to live among humans. Living so, She would
understand the joys and sorrows of mortal life and increase Her
wisdom when humans called on Her for help.

So one day Kuan Yin came to live as the youngest daughter
of three in a house with a cruel father. He ignored his daughters
for years, and when he didn't ignore them he spoke coldly to
them. When they came of age, he became openly mean. "I'm
tired of you," he raged. "Marry, every one of you. Find your-
selves husbands. Stay in their houses, not mine. You are not
welcome here."

The eldest daughter married a silent warrior. The second
married a greedy merchant. But Kuan Yin said, "I do not wish
to marry. I am going to live in the Temple of the White Bird,
the temple of gold and black marble with lotus flowers in the
fountain."

When Kuan Yin continued to refuse to marry, Her father arranged for the women in the temple to treat Kuan Yin cruelly. "Make her do all the hardest work," he said. "Pull Her hair, and give Her only dry bread and water to eat. Then She will leave the temple and marry, as I command."

Some women at the temple were afraid, and they obeyed Kuan Yin's father. They gave Her the hardest work and not enough food. But Kuan Yin waited until all the others slept. Then the serpent came to help Her carry the water. The tiger appeared and gathered wood for the fire. The birds flew about busily collecting vegetables from the garden. The spirit of the fire rose up and helped to cook the food. The peacock even swept the kitchen floor with his thousand-eyed tail.

The father was so enraged when he heard of the animals helping Kuan Yin that he set fire to the Temple of the White Bird. "Now every woman who dares defy me will die!" he screamed.

But Kuan Yin came and put out the fire with Her own hands. When Her father saw that not only was the temple safe, but Kuan Yin's hands were not even blistered, his rage knew no bounds.

"Find Her and cut off Her head!" he ordered his servant.

The servant was amazed when his sword broke in two instead of harming the body of Kuan Yin. But the servant was afraid to fail in the task of killing Kuan Yin. So he squeezed Her throat with his hands until She couldn't breathe and tied Her lifeless body to the back of a tiger, setting it loose in the jungle.

The Land of the Dead was dark, and Kuan Yin was afraid. But soon She sat up and began to sing. You know the songs She sang. The ones with the melodies that comfort and bring the sleep of renewal. The people who lived in the Land of the Dead gathered around Kuan Yin. They looked at Kuan Yin in wonder, and then they began to take each other's hands. They touched Her robes and began to chant and sing. The pain and the loneliness they felt melted and there came peace and joy.

The King of the Dead was furious. "No singing in this place," he thundered. "Begone!" And he banished Kuan Yin from the Kingdom of Death.

So Kuan Yin returned to Earth and Her soul rejoined Her body. Quietly She made her way to an island in the northeastern sea. There She lives to this day, chanting and singing for the well-being of all in the Land of the Living and the Land of the Dead and comforting us in our troubles with Her sacred willow branch when we call out Her name.

Sedna (SAID-nuh)
The Great Woman at the Bottom of the Sea
(Inuit People)

Introduction

S edna, also known as Arnaknagsak and Neqivik, has probably a dozen different names, depending on the language
spoken in Greenland, Alaska, northern Canada, and the islands
between. Sedna's country is the severe and beautiful land of the
Inuit peoples, often called by outsiders Eskimos. Though a
giver of life and abundance, Her good is not to be worshiped:
it is sufficient unto itself. Rather, Her people placate Her vig-
ilantly in order that Her power rest on the side of plenty and
safety rather than barrenness and danger. Her people trust in
the wisdom of Her placaters, the medicine people and the
storytellers—the angakok—for they are the seers who have
touched the helping spirits with their souls.

Evil is real to the Inuit peoples. Daily they face great darkness, storms, gales, and stealthy fog. Despite the convenience of
ready-made tools and electricity, the experience of generations
shows that life is difficult: humans constantly confront forces

stronger than ourselves. Sedna embodies the innocence and the clarity, the evil and the good. From Her depth emanates the mysterious regulations of Life, which include the matter-of-fact necessity of Death.

Depending on Her pleasure, Sedna is the Goddess who keeps back and sends out animals for the hunt, and to Her She gathers all spirits who die of natural causes.

I blended themes from more than one Inuit myth for Sedna's story. This Goddess helps me come to terms with sacrifice and with the tremendous shifts of life, so great that for the Inuit peoples they must be marked with an entire change of name. I have invoked Her with seawater and a wooden comb.

How the People Came to Eat in Wintertime

HE ANGAKOK are the special ones. They can converse with the Sun and the Moon. They travel to the Underworld, going through rocks if need be. Indeed, the angakok know the way to the floor of the ocean. That is why they are able to tell the story of Sedna, the Great Woman Who Lives at the Bottom of the Sea. They tell of Her before the change in Her calling name, when She was young and lived only on the land. And they tell of Her now, whose mercy and abundance we beg, soft and generous when we appease Her by combing Her flowing raven hair.

In the old days, say the angakok, when the Sun Dogs never tired of pulling the Sun across the sky, before humans came to Earth, Sedna was the beautiful, flat-nosed Land Maiden called Avilayoq (a-VEE-luh-yoke). Avilayoq lived among caribou, musk ox, reindeer, hare, fox, and the birds of the air. When Sedna was Avilayoq, say the angakok, the land knew only daytime. The Goddess then, for centuries at a time, would beat the frame of her ayayut drum and croon the song of the Land Maiden. Handsome, free, and graceful was She: Eyaya-eya. Eyaya-eya.

Other times, She would sit on a rock, dressed in Her most lovely clothes, quite still and staring out over land and sea, gazing for eons at the bottomless placid water that reflected the glowing colors of the Sun hung red, yellow, and low in the sky. Silent and motionless, Avilayoq would drink in the rays of the Sun broken into blue, green, and blinding white by the breaking, floating icebergs.

At other times, say the angakok, Avilayoq had the heart of a child at play with a ball. She skipped at the edge of the sea and teased the strong, persistent First Sun Dog, who lay his compliments so prettily at Her enticingly booted feet. The day came, though, when Avilayoq saw that the eyes of First Sun Dog were flecked with kindness, and the tease in Her heart turned to thrill.

Earth was never the same again, say the angakok, when Avilayoq took First Dog as Her husband. Avilayoq and Sun Dog built a snow hut to lie in, and the other Sun Dogs, leaderless now, rested in such a way that night came for the first time to the land of endless day. And out of the womb of Avilayoq came human beings: small and large of every age. They too began to make huts and to hunt for food on a land that was fast turning colder than Avilayoq had ever known before.

There had always been snow and ice, but now came an ominous thundering of that ice, louder than the beating of a thousand ayayuts. A violence of snow driving off the sea sent caribou and musk ox so deep into the freezing night that none could follow.

Gone was the laughter, the plenty, the Sun. Come was the time of no eating, and the wails of Her people filled the ears of Avilayoq. The heart of Avilayoq, say the angakok, grew heavy as a carcass. She wrung Her hands for the fate of Her humans. Then the picture of the quiet gazing of that endless summer filled Her, and there was born in Avilayoq a plan that filled Her both with peace and dread.

Avilayoq called Her people to Her. "You must gather the strength you have left," She called over the howling of the wind. "You must build a boat of skins. In that boat I will ride with the Old Man out into the sea. There will I calm this sky and call back the summer's food."

Weak as they were, the people were amazed. No one before had left the land for the waters. And to call back the summer's food! Eyaya-eya! Eyaya-eya!

The people built a boat of skins. Avilayoq dressed again in Her finest clothes. To Sun Dog She said, "Life is heavier than death. It so happens that one is leaving."

"Are You leaving now?" asked Sun Dog, and though His eyes were filled with sorrow, He did not follow Her.

Bent and falling, Avilayoq with the Old Man pulled themselves to the edge of the sea where the kayak waited tied to a bone stuck in the Earth. Avilayoq and the Old Man climbed inside, and the Old Man cut the boat free with his axe.

The kayak rolled in the black waves like an eye in the head of a wounded caribou. The silhouette of Avilayoq stood tall, arms outstretched in the shrieking gray torrent. Avilayoq shouted, say the angakok. She begged the sky and the sea that had beckoned Her so long ago. But what happened next, say the angakok, is horrible to relate. No one knows why—some say it was a frenzy of terror—no one knows why, but the arms of the Old Man shoved. They shoved the Land Maiden into the pitching sea.

Avilayoq writhed against the icy cold that knifed Her body. Her hands tore upward at the edge of the kayak, but the Old Man took up his axe and cut off the grasping fingers of the Goddess.

With a terrible scream, the head of Avilayoq sank into the waters of the deep.

It was then, say the angakok, that the fine clothes of the Land Maiden slipped forever from Her huge, beautiful body. Her hair, ripped from its hood, floated like wings about Her. It was then that the severed fingers of Avilayoq changed to seals, to walrus, to polar bears and whales. It was the body and blood of Avilayoq that gave the water animals to Her people that they might hunt and eat also in Winter.

It was then, say the angakok, that the Land Maiden, now the Great Woman of the Sea, took the new calling name of Sedna. As Sedna, She lies at the bottom of the sea in Her house like the houses of people. It is She we fear and She who gives forth all abundance.

But the thanklessness and broken promises of people, they say, collect like grease and dirt in Her hair that Her own hands are now unable to groom. It is by righting the wrongs of land and sea that we content Her by running the comb of diligence, patience, and frugality through the sheets of Her wild black hair.

IV

The Force of Life:
Sexuality and Creativity

Desire turns the wheel of life on Earth. Moon fancies the swell of the sea. Twilight waits, eyes soft, for the night. Birds nest again and again because they ache after flight. The artist speaks of having to create, of holding inside her something that she must express, the thing in her that leaps after life. And surely as a diver braves the depths of the fantastically imaged sea, the artist plumbs her own deep for the treasure she then midwifes to air.

We give birth to ourselves over and over again. Before the birthings are the gestations. Before the gestations come the matings. Before the matings, the courtings and before them virginities. After the birthings, we grow, we lose, we mourn; we are babies all over again. Then, even as we cling to the breast, the cells in us bound after childhood.

Desire pulses at the center of Earth-centered spirituality. In Goddess consciousness, the sexual is sacred. In this ancient, new religion we are remaking together, worship means savoring, delighting, preserving, luxuriating. In Goddess consciousness we animate the grass and the water in the way we, delicious and sly, give name and personality to a lover's genitals.

In this religion, we indeed "follow our bliss," as historian of religion Joseph Campbell said.

When sexuality is sacred, creativity—not compliance—is our attitude toward external reality. When we relate creatively and playfully to our world, we minimize the experience of feeling caught in someone else's mechanizations. When we play and create, we are alive in space and time. Wishes and objects intersect. Whole spectra of feeling replace the sense of futility.

Sexuality in Goddess consciousness is far broader than feelings about reproductive functions or even purely pleasurable sexual acts or choices. Goddess sexuality is a metaphor for what we yearn for and devote ourselves to—not out of duty but rather ardor and zeal. Sexuality is the way we are intimate with our own feeling states; the way we are moved by the diamonds of rain on a spider web; our paintings and letters; our laughter and stews; our persuasions and politics. Sexuality is our moment-by-moment, changing relish for who we are. Sexuality is our willingness to let ourselves really show in the world.

Even before the purposeful revival of Goddess consciousness, people had begun to long for the kind of bodily state that would resacralize our beings. Free love and the drug culture were both mass attempts to break control-culture's bondage. "Love! Not war!" we cried in the time of Vietnam's napalm, thus correctly tying the new relaxation of sexual mores to a fervor for creation and life on ecopolitical levels. "Be here now!" we chanted as drugs encouraged us to drop the inner nagging that cemented together our pressured lives. But "free love" and "being here now" in a culture that trashes Earth with plastics and poisons and practices the "isms" of injustice are doomed to perpetuate the terrible chasm between our bodies' truths and our spiritualities. In the culture of control, other people and our own experiences become objects to collect and consume. When we wield power over another and find ourselves in power-under positions, our creativity and ability to preserve become slaves to what can be bought and taken. Instead of being filled with sacred feeling, we are left struggling to conceal from ourselves how much we have wasted and thrown away.

But the consciousness of the Goddess is uncovering the waste. Over the chasm between our bodies and our souls, we are building a bridge of equal partnership between what we consume and what we nurture. In Goddess consciousness we do not pretend that life contains no death. We honor the reality that the preservation of our own lives requires death—of plants and animals and minerals. We are frugal and mindful about our consumption. Nor do we pretend that death contains no life: we reuse and use again the endless cycle of our waste.

In Goddess consciousness, we are inventing new ways of relating the feminine to the masculine. Everywhere in Nature are both forces. Nearly every kind of reproduction involves both the yang and the yin. Whether in homo-, hetero-, or autosexuality, we sense both masculine and feminine powers at work. The masculine of the control culture, however, has dominated our inner and outer lives. The feminine overpowered, we have been caused to lead lives disconnected with our souls and our abilities to be human "beings" instead of human "doings," as psychologist-writer John Bradshaw has said.

In Goddess mythologies, the Great Female often has a Male Consort. The consort or lover of the Goddess, sometimes also Her brother or son, is ready, devoted, and adoring. He is strong, full, and ever-changing in His own right, but it is the Goddess Who is central. Her lover enters Her temple by invitation and with thanksgiving.

A sprained ankle several months ago and a cane I used to help me walk became wonderful metaphors for the Goddess and Her Consort in my life. When the speed of my life sapped away with the purple and pain of my foot, I found I existed, like the Goddess Herself, in majestic slowness. And, like Her Consort, my cane was strong and available at my need: only together could we make the trip to the mailbox. Ancient and present in my body as I was, supported and safe with my cane, I was not efficient, but I was alive. I watched a leaf fall and the clouds make gray gardens in the sky.

Here was a partnership of feminine and masculine—the

cane useless without me, my body needing its simple reliability. Earth-centered spirituality, I am convinced, asks of us a similar partnership. Outer technology must be in service of the sacred well-being of our living Planet.

Huitaca (whee-TAH-kah)
Queen of Pleasure
(Chibcha People)

Introduction

L ike other original peoples of the Americas, the Chibcha of Colombia may have roots in northern Asia from which as many as 42,000 years ago they are thought to have crossed the Bering Strait into Alaska, reaching South America by 6000 B.C.E. The Chibcha worship the Divine Ancestress Bachue, Whom they envision as both Woman and Snake. Bachue is Teacher of Peace and Order and Protector of Agriculture for the Chibcha, a role similar to that of Isis, Demeter, and Lamia (see stories) for Their peoples.

Like peoples the world over, the Chibcha picture the Great Mother in many ways. Huitaca is the aspect of the Great Mother who is Queen of Love and Pleasure. She is the Owl Moon Woman, Who cradles the rites of renewal and creation. The Chibcha pose Her wisdom against that of the wandering Bochica, the masculine deity responsible for the teaching of spinning, weaving, and industry.

108

I wrote this myth for Huitaca in order to invoke the sense of "Goddess time" that has grown in lovely counterpoint to the production-oriented hustle of the city world in which I live. The hurried buying and selling for profit that the European-influenced world takes so for granted are hilarious (and tragic) distortions of human energy to peoples for whom Earth is alive. Present-day original peoples in Australia (the Australoids), for example, understand production in a completely different way than does the culture of control. The Australoids trade not for profit, but for symmetry. Goods are malign in and of themselves; they work against their possessors unless they are constantly in motion. Goods for the Australoids are tokens of intention: to trade, to meet again, to fix frontiers, to intermarry, to sing and dance, and to share ideas and resources. From this viewpoint, production of goods loses its tyranny and instead integrates into its rhythm personal, social, and spiritual well-being. Bruce Chatwin's *The Songlines* outlines this understanding of Australoid trade.

Huitaca, for me, Goddess of perfume and feasting, music and love, is certainly also Goddess of the luxurious world that unfolds before me when I remove the clamp of the clock and listen, instead, to the lilt of my own bloodstream.

The Clock That Was Really an Egg

I N ANCIENT times, the people of a certain village lived close to their Goddess Huitaca. Always She was in their midst, and it was due to Her presence that the people lived as if every day were someone's birthday, which, of course, it was. The people of the village worked hard. But if they were tired, they rested completely. If they were hungry, they ate. And they never made a bowl or a basket or a boat or a blanket without adding the finest colors and pictures they could imagine. The people strove to make the objects of their effort reflect the beauty of their Goddess. So they sewed the birds and the sky onto their clothes, and grasses and rivers blew on their berry pots. When the people of the village lived close to Huitaca, they lived with feeling under their skins.

In those days, just anytime at all, the people made music. "Huitaca!" they called. "Come with bananas and bangles on Your braids! Huitaca! Come dance with us!" Then into reeds the people blew, and onto drums they beat. The seeds of gourds shook, shook, shook, and in color and singing the feet and bodies of the people stamped and swayed. Eyes shone and mouths drank dark pink juice and skins gleamed with sweat diamonds.

Huitaca whirled in the center fast as fire, and Her chants spun men to men, men to women, women to each other, and back again the other way. Huitaca laughed and whooped and panted. Her people clapped and hugged and leapt.

Sometimes when the reed blowers slept and the fruits lay sucked dry near the spent honey-wine skin, Huitaca lay quiet with Her people and looked at the sky. During the day, the villagers and their Goddess found animals in the clouds. In the night, they cooled themselves under the scarves of shimmers that were the stars.

Huitaca was the bringer of perfume and play, jewelry and ornaments, soaps and oils, touching and love. When the people of the village lived close to Huitaca, they lived with feeling under their skins.

One day came the beginning of a big change in the village. Bochica arrived that day. Since he was a stranger—and a tall and strong one—the people gathered around him. Bochica had something the people had never seen before. It was small and round, with markings around the edge. "Is it an egg?" the people asked, touching the markings they thought were funny-shaped speckles. No, it was a clock, Bochica told them. He explained how the clock could measure out minutes and hours and days. "What's that good for?" the people wanted to know.

Bochica seemed surprised. "What's it good for?" he asked. "Why, without this clock, you can't make enough things to sell and buy."

"What's sell and buy?" asked the people.

Bochica shook his head. Now he seemed really surprised. "Look," he said. "You own a few things now, right?"

"Right," said the people.

"Well, if you had a lot more things, you could take them to the next village and get money for them, and with that money you can buy even more things!"

The people shook their heads this time. "We have enough things," they said. But they allowed Bochica to stay in the village with his clock and to make a home there. Every time the people called to their Goddess Huitaca, Bochica shook his head. "Huitaca with Her bangles and bananas," he muttered. "What good is all this music when there is work to do?"

Time passed, and Bochica continued to tell the people how fine it would be to sell and buy. For a long time, the people didn't listen to Bochica. "With Huitaca, we have all we need," they told him. "We're afraid your clock would make us forget that."

After a while, though, the people began to listen. They listened so much, in fact, that they did begin to forget Huitaca. They stopped putting oils and perfumes on their skins, and they didn't remember that every day was someone's birthday.

On the day the people decided to make Bochica their leader, Huitaca let out a cry. "Whoooooo?" She called out, and it sounded like a moan. When no one heard Her, She turned Herself into an Owl and flew away.

No one noticed, except one little girl. "Mama, I saw Huitaca turn Herself into an Owl and fly into Bochica's egg," said the little girl to her mother. "Shhhhh, child," said her mother. "Besides, that's a clock, not an egg."

"Bochica will make a fine leader," the people told each other. "He's tall and strong, and his clock will help us make enough things to sell and buy."

The people didn't know how the clock would help make things for them, but they soon found out. The clock told Bochica what time it was, and Bochica told the people when to work and when to stop and when to eat and when to sleep. Bochica walked all day among the people with his clock.

"That wall is taking too long," said Bochica. "Hurry up."

"But, Bochica, we're painting beautiful pictures on it," said the people.

"While you're wasting time on pictures," he said, "you could be making things to sell in the next village. Time to move on!"

Bochica thought that if every day is a birthday, that just means all the days are alike. "No need to have a party on an ordinary day, now, is there?" he said. "Too much work to do." And he strode by, telling people not to dawdle, to get busy, and to wake up.

Bochica never liked it either if someone made something he didn't know the name of. "We're making things to sell," he'd say. "Who's going to buy that thing, if they don't even know what it's called?"

Many years went by. For a long time people remembered when they had laughed and danced and made music. Sometimes they even tried to call Huitaca, just like in the old days. But She never came, and Bochica got angry if he heard them calling Her or trying to make music. So after a while the only one who thought a lot about Huitaca was the little girl who'd seen Her change into an Owl. That little girl grew up and told her daughter the story. That daughter grew up and told *her* little girl the story.

By this time, too, Bochica was old. He looked pinched in the face and very thin. Late one hot afternoon, even Bochica got tired. "I'll sit down under this tree for just a minute," he said to himself. He carefully set his clock beside him and then fell asleep. Bochica began to snore.

A little girl picking berries nearby looked up when she heard Bochica snoring. She saw his clock beside him.

Now this was the very same little girl whose mother and grandmother had told her the story of Huitaca the Owl flying into the clock. So she wasn't at all surprised to find, when she crept very close, that the clock looked just like an egg. She touched it with one finger. The egg clock was warm and pretty. The little girl picked up the egg in both hands.

Certainly the little girl meant to take that clock to her mother, to show her how very much like an egg it looked. But in a second, the little girl had dropped that egg clock, and with a whirring of wings and a great "Whoooooooooo!" Huitaca Herself flew out of the cracked pieces on the ground.

"Whooooooooo! Whooooooooo!" sounded Huitaca.

People were so busy they didn't notice at first. But the little girl began to run. "Huitaca! That's Who!" she yelled. "Huitaca!"

"Whoooooooo, whooooooo," said Huitaca as She circled above the village.

People began to look up from their work. Their spines began to tingle.

"Huitaca!" called the little girl. "Huitaca! It's Your birthday!" Then, just like in the old story her mother had told her, the girl called, "Huitaca! Come with bananas and bangles on Your braids! Huitaca! Come dance with us!"

People stopped working. They looked at their hands and stretched their necks. They arched their backs and began to smile. People began to move. A man broke off a reed and began to blow it. Another turned over a pot and began to beat it. The seeds in gourds began to shake, shake, shake, and a ribbon of color and song began to form under the people's patting feet.

Bochica woke up. "My clock!" he cried out. He gathered the broken pieces to his chest. "Back to work!" he yelled. But no one heard in the swirl of music.

A chain of dancers pounded by, and the women scooped up the numbers from the clock to decorate their hair. The stars on the scarf of the sky began to sugar the night. With a great flapping of wings, Huitaca took Woman form again, and Her braids stood straight out as She whirled fast as fire at the center of Her people.

After that night, the people of the village never again forgot Huitaca. They did not forget Bochica, either, with his selling and buying. But once again, they took the time they needed to reflect the beauty of their Goddess in the things they made. No more work without making music. No more eating and sleeping only when it was time to eat and sleep. They ate when they were hungry and rested when they were tired. The people began to live again as if every day were someone's birthday, which, of course, it was. The people began to live again with feeling under their skins.

Athena (uh-THEEN-uh)
Mother of Invention
(Greece)

Introduction

As Athena Parthenia, She Who Comes from Herself, the Holy Virgin of Athens metamorphosed Her form and name in the myths of an array of cultures. Like Lamia (see story), She rose up in the land the Greeks called Libya, what we know today as all of North Africa, except for Egypt. Called Neith, Anath, and Ath-enna, She was the Triple Goddess whose tremendous powers came to hold a special fascination for even patriarchal storytellers. Rather than obliterate Her name, these tellers instead stripped from Her the associations of Moon, Snake, and Owl that encapsulated Her Woman mysteries. They invented the tale of Her birth from the male God Zeus's head, and in dramas of war and strategy they dressed Her in helmet and sword and placed in Her mouth words that scorned women.

Misogyny could not obscure, however, the essence of clear-mindedness that is Athena's special gift of fertility. Artist of

115

real-world crafts, Athena, the Great Weaver, came to embody the complex skills of planning and follow through in domestic and political arenas. Hers was the might of civilization itself.

I wrote this new myth for Athena in honor of plumbing, the stupendous, invisible weaving of pipes beneath every city, without which vast numbers of people living closely together cannot healthily function. As Queen of Sanitation Engineering, Athena is similar to the Roman Cloaca, an aspect of Juno (see story), who was Queen of Sewers and Excrement. Athena, called Minerva by the Romans, Empress of Architectural Brilliance, is the Goddess I call on to help me plan, edit, and organize. It has been enormously important to me to return this masculinized realm to the Great Mother. That act, on a cultural scale, will begin to heal the shocking damage that invariably results when we split production from consequence and use from waste.

The Weaving of the Streets and Plumbing

HE GODDESS
Athena got up in the morning and tied an apartment house onto
each foot. She climbed into Her skirt made of hospitals and
libraries and pulled a shirt of towers over Her head. She belted
Her waist and tied back Her hair with two pillars. Into Her
pockets She stuffed streets and pipes.

Today was the day to finish Her two great tapestries. Today in the cities, She would weave the last of Her mighty
threads. First She pulled the streets from Her pocket. Bending
and turning, She poked and pressed them into the huge grid of
roads She had made.

Then She walked down into the Earth. There gleamed the
net of pipes She had strung down the walls of the buildings,
under the halls, past the steel and brick foundations. From every tub, every sink, and every toilet angled the pipes, curving
and pointing out to the sea. Under the Earth, Athena squatted.

117

Using the last of Her pipes from Her pocket, she measured, chopped, and screwed them until they fit just so.

The people had gathered. Hundreds waited on foot and with carts at the sides of Her roads. Hundreds waited at the edge of the sea beside the huge vats that would catch the waters of Athena's pipe weaving. Hundreds stood high on the mountain where the waters began.

Athena climbed out of the Earth and stood at the center of the cities where all could see Her. She loosed the pillar from Her hair, and a rush of air lifted the mass of it and settled it into the clouds.

"It is finished!" Athena shouted. "My tapestries are finished!"

The people cheered.

"Now hear the story of My tapestries," said Athena.

The people listened.

"My roads I call My transportation tapestry," said Athena. Her voice was loud and strong. "Without the streets of My tapestry, your travel is clumsy and long. With My streets, your travel is easy. With My streets, your travel is free of rocks and thorns. When you visit and work or gather and carry, you go straight and true to each other."

The people waved branches and raised their voices. They tossed flowers by the thousands into Athena's great transportation tapestry.

Athena spoke again. "I call My pipe tapestry plumbing," She said. "My plumbing carries away your wastes and your filth. Without my plumbing your cities stink and are full of disease. With My plumbing, your cities are clean and your air fresh."

The people clamored at their beautiful Athena. They called Her name and cheered. Then the man who stood at the great spigot at the top of the mountain waved a white cloth high.

"We are ready, Athena!" the man yelled. He raised his huge hammer. "We are ready to start the waters flowing in Your great plumbing tapestry!"

"Wait!" thundered Athena. "You are not ready!"

118

The people stirred. They looked at each other. The man at the spigot lowered his hammer.

Athena held out Her hands. "My people," She said. "You have not heard the end of My story."

The people waited.

"Today," said Athena, "you are grateful for My gifts to you. Today you fill my roads with flowers. Today you sing the praises of Athena, the Great Road Maker and Plumber."

"But," She rumbled, "there will come a time when you will forget. There will come a day when you will forget that your roads and your plumbing are Mine. There will come a day when you will want to abuse My weavings."

The people raised their voices in disbelief.

"Silence," said Athena. Then Her shoulders drooped. But Her voice was still strong. "There will come a day, My children, when you will build fast machines that spew out poison into the air over My roads. You will dump poison at My roadsides. There will come a day, My children, when you will pour poison into My plumbing. 'We can't see it,' you will say. 'So what does it matter?' That is the day you will forget to clean the waters of My plumbing before they pour into the sea."

Athena hung Her head. The people were silent. They shook their heads. They could not imagine forgetting the Great Weaver or Her gifts. Then a woman cried out, "Athena! We will not forget."

Athena lifted Her head. The people took up the cry. "Athena! We will not forget!" they shouted. "We will tell our children. And our children will tell their grandchildren."

Athena's shoulders straightened. She took two steps, and the Earth shook under Her weight. She stretched out Her arms and cupped one hand around the people on the mountain. She cupped Her right hand about the people at the edge of the sea. The people at the sides of Her roads pressed together.

"My children," said Athena, and Her voice was like a thousand harp strings. "See that you do not forget. See that you do not forget that the tapestries are Mine."

"Never!" cried the people. "We will never forget!"

119

Athena smiled. "Then we are ready," She said. "Turn the faucet."

The man at the spigot on the mountain threw his whole weight into the hammer blow that turned the giant faucet. Again and again he hammered, and then the water began to flow. A trickle at first and then a roar of white and blue filled the coppers and silvers of Athena's great plumbing tapestry.

The people began to dance in Athena's streets.

Athena held Her fists in the air.

Inside the buildings, the sounds of flushing and splashing gurgled forth. Dishes sparkled and babies patted hands into warm baths. "Never forget, never forget," patted the babies' hands.

Outside the buildings, the carts moved to and fro on the crisscross streets. "Never forget," squeaked the axles. "Never forget," fluttered the birds.

"Never forget," hummed the people at the vats at the edge of the sea.

"Never forget," dreamed the waves and the fishes and the long green hair of the plants at the bottom of the sea.

Bridget (BRIDGE-it)
Inventor of Writing
(Ireland)

Introduction

I mpossible to banish, the Great Goddess Danu (see story) later took the human-divine form of the Goddess Bridget and finally accepted the status of sainthood, conferred on Her by Pope Gregory I. The pope told Augustine in the sixth century C.E. to co-opt rather than destroy the pagan sites and customs of the newly evangelized Celtic peoples. The church thus added the new Saint Bridget to the nativity scene, calling Her midwife to the Virgin Mary. They changed the name of Her Holy Imbolg, February 1, to Candlemas, only thinly disguising with the trappings of Christianity its pagan reverence for the union of light and land.

But Irish writers, refusing absolutely to diabolize their Goddess or even fully to accept Her "sainthood," insisted on calling Her Queen of Heaven, and they identified Her with the Christian Mother of God.

Certainly their Bridget, Triple Goddess of the Celtic empire of Brigantia, which included parts of the British Isles, Spain, and France, was once known as Mother of All Life. Identified with the Changing Moon and associated with ox (a later nativity scene prop), boar, and ram, Bridget also personified the entire kingdom. She conferred prosperity on a king only when She ritually accepted him as Her spouse. Her sacred count was nineteen, the number of years it takes for the New Moon to coincide with the Sun's Winter Solstice. Her priestesses, too, numbered nineteen; for centuries their generations kept Her sacred fire burning in Kildare, Ireland.

To this day, the custom of fashioning Bridget's cross is widespread. In honor of Her fertility, people in the Gaelic-rooted parts of the isles weave, of rushes or straw, three- or four-armed crosses on the first day of spring, the time of preparation for the first planting. Though its precise meaning is lost in antiquity, the cross may well symbolize the sacred union of the powers above and below.

Adored of poets and giver of medicine, smithcraft, and writing, Bridget, Queen Earth Herself, wears the cloak of Catholicism with regal nonchalance. Her story is adapted from the one told in *Ancient Mirrors of Womanhood* by Merlin Stone.

I call on Bridget on February 1 or 2 when the first bright weeds have burst through the ground after winter rains. I pot a new houseplant every year at this time in honor of the project or quality I have resolved to make part of my life in the next year. I also feel Her presence when I drink two cups of mugwort tea midcycle each month to bring my blood easily.

Queen of the Four Fires

LONG TIME ago, at the first crack of pink in a young morning, the Goddess Bridget was born. Out of Her head rose a column of fire that stretched to the very sky. While the Nine Sisters who had helped to birth Her crooned and swayed in a circle around Her, Bridget broke off a flaming plume from Her column of fire and dropped it on the circle of ground before Her. It blew big and red there on the hearth.

Then Bridget reached both hands into the crackling heat, took a piece of the fire, and swallowed it. The fire She ate went straight to her heart.

There stood the Goddess Bridget, fire leaping from Her head, licking up inside Her heart, shooting from Her hands, and dancing on the hearth before Her.

About Her hearth, Bridget built a chimney of brick. About the chimney, She built a roof of thatch and walls of stone. In that way the Goddess made Herself a house, and in it She keeps Her great fires, which have served Her people forevermore.

From the fire on Bridget's head came writing and poetry. From the fire in Bridget's heart came the warmth of compassion. From the fire on Bridget's hands came the craft of bending iron. And from the fires of Bridget's hearth and the waters of Her magic well came the healing teas.

Word of Bridget's fire gifts spread far and wide. People flocked to learn from Bridget the secret of using fire to soften iron and bend it to the shapes of their desires. Bending iron was called smithcraft, and the people made wheels, pots, and tools of iron and clucked their tongues at the wonder of it all.

Bridget collected in Her house all the medicine plants of the Earth. With them, She made healing teas, for which the people begged the recipes. In huge iron pots Bridget boiled the waters from Her well on Her hearth fires. When the bubbles were high, She'd take the pots from the fires, add the special leaves and barks and roots, and cover the pots to steep out the herbal powers.

She gave a boy with bad teeth the tea of the dandelion root to make his teeth strong. She gave a young woman raspberry leaf tea to help her womb carry its child. When an old man gasped with pain at Her house, a cane in each hand to help him walk, Bridget gave him wintergreen bark for the pain and black cherry juice for the healing. To a little girl with a broken leg, She gave comfrey to knit her bone sound again. When a grandmother said, "I'm drying up, Bridget. It hurts to get old," Bridget brewed motherwort, licorice root, and dried parsley. "Cup a day for you, Grandmother," said Bridget, giving the woman the tea and a basket of eggs.

Once two men with the terrible sores of leprosy came to Bridget. "Bathe yourself in My well," said Bridget to the first man. At every place Bridget's waters touched, the man's skin turned whole again. "Now bathe your friend," said Bridget. But the newly healed man could not bear the sight of his friend. Repulsed, he backed away. "I cannot touch him," he said to Bridget. "Then you are not truly healed," said Bridget. And

She gave the first man back his leprosy and healed the second man. "Return to Me with compassion," She said to the first man, putting Her hand on his heart. "There find your healing."

The people wanted to tell everyone about Bridget's wisdom and Her medicines. "But we can't remember which plants You use for which sicknesses or where You gather them or how long You steep them," they told Bridget. Bridget took a blackened stick from the fire and began to make marks with it on a flat piece of bark. "These are the talking marks," She said. "They are the way to remember what you don't want to forget." The fire on Bridget's head blazed up as She wrote.

Every year at midwinter the people stop to give thanks to Bridget. "Thank You, Queen Bridget, for the talking marks. Thank You for compassion. Thank You for the smithcraft. Thank You for Your fires of head, heart, hands, and hearth."

Shakti (SHOCK-tee)
Queen of the Cosmos
(India)

Introduction

The Goddess Shakti's name translates as "Cosmic Energy."
In India's Hinduism, She is the dominant force of the
universe. (See stories of Devi, Maya, and Kali, other forms of
the Shakti.) She alone has the power to move the dormant male
force to action, and a God without His Shakti is helpless. The
Shakti is time, the cosmic tension and activity that brings the
corpse of eternity to life over and over again. Shiva, Her consort, is that Eternal Dancer who comes to life in Her arms. It
is in relationship to Her that the God Shiva expresses the essence of His character. He creates, maintains, destroys, con-
ceals, and favors, all at Her will, multiplying Himself into
endless actors, like vapor, coming to pass, to flow, and to van-
ish. Tantric Hinduism worships the sexual principle as a metaphor for life itself. Life's energies of water, Earth, and snake
are embodied by the Shakti's Yoni, or sacred Vulva. The Shiva's Lingam, or sacred Phallus, embodies the energies of fire,

Sun, and eagle. As in the Central American Goddess Mayahuel's relationship to Snake-the-Wind (see story), this mythology poses none of the West's opposition between snake and Sun (Devil and God), but instead it honors the union of differences as the ultimate power of the universe.

The Shakti and Her Shiva together enable the dance at the center of the universe. This center is within each human heart. The Western mystical system called alchemy, which concerns itself with the substance and transformation of the soul, honors this same universal heart center, and uses extensive sexual imagery. The chant *om* or *aum*, made popular in the United States by students of the East in the 1960s and '70s, recapitulates the spectrum of worldly states represented by the Tantric Goddess and Her Consort. *A* is the state of waking consciousness in the world of gross experience. *U* is the state of dreaming consciousness. *M* is the state of dreamless, blissful sleep; undifferentiated nonexperience. The pause of silence that follows *aum* is the ultimate unmanifestation of divine reality.

The dance of the God Shiva is far better known than the inspiration of His Shakti. Discovering the Shakti gave me great satisfaction. I wrote the story of the Shakti in order to invoke the tremendously private feeling I have about these two cosmic forces.

The Shakti and the Shiva at the Center of the Human Heart

TOOK MY SISTER.
I took my son. I took my lover. I took my friend. But in the end
I had to go alone to the center of my heart. At first I said, let's
not waste time. And anyway I am afraid. I want a hand to hold.

But I had to go alone. I went alone, I'm telling you. Yet
when I got to the center, I was not alone. For the Shakti and
Her Shiva were there.

Past the teachings and the wishings I went, under the cor-
rections and the rules. I moved through the kaleidoscope of my
world. The wind brushed my ears; the sun colored me hot. The
rains came. I traveled past the jeweled elephants and the purple
curtains of principles and politics. I turned through the spiral of
peacocks and calves, under the castle entwined with roses and
long green rice. I swam under the fan of the lotus into the warm
black mud of the roots. I floated. I floated down to the deep.

The silence there was like a cape. I could feel the eye in my mind close in peace, and I sang the song of nothing without any words.

Then I heard the sound of *aaaaa* around me. The eye in my mind darted open. I could see I'd come to a red velvet room. Inside stood a bed hung with silk. But I could not go in, for two black tigers paced its entrance. Two black tigers—one striped yellow and the other white. I recoiled. I wished for my friend. I pressed away and the sound of *aaaaa* pressed back on me. I saw the mouths of the tigers yawn. Their teeth and scalloped lips glinted wet.

I snapped shut the eye in my mind. The sound of *uuuuu* came to me. When I opened that eye again, behold! The tigers, first the yellow, then the white, scratched their spines against the floor, forepaws limp with pleasure, and the fur of their bellies rumpled and soft. That sound of *uuuuu* clasped me tight, and I was able now to enter the room. There the Shakti and Her Shiva held each other on the flower-strewn bed.

I was shy. Surely this embrace was not meant for my eyes. But I stared. The blue blacks of their heads looked like rocks in a moving river. I felt the sweeping longing and fascination of a child. Oh! I knew I must go.

But the Shiva sat up. "Stay!" He said. The movements of his chest and wrist were graceful as a cat's.

"This is the center of your heart, after all," said the Shakti. Her eyes were laughing, and She'd hooked a hand over the rosy blanket at Her neck. "Stay and let Us tell you Our story."

Shiva patted the bed and inclined a welcome with His eyes and chin.

I held my breath.

"Come," said the Shakti. Both Her arms reached out to me.

I scrambled.

And there I was between Them smelling Their jasmine and patchouli, enveloped like a yolk in an egg. The sound of *mmmmm* swelled around me—*mmmmm*—and I slept.

When I awoke, I traced with my finger the design imprinted on my forearm by the cuddle of covers. There, while I lay tiny between Them, They told me Their story.

"At the beginning of every beginning," said the Shakti, "I am alone. There is nothing. I am like a windless red flag, vibrant with color but not moving. And I watch My Lord Shiva. The lashes on His cheeks are so pointed and fine. His cheeks are like wax. He is so still, then. So unbelievably still."

"She says I look dead," said the Shiva.

"You do, You look dead. There is nothing. So I drift and I float. I lie with Myself and I dream," said the Shakti.

"And then, finally, She wakes Me," said the Shiva.

"Yes, I want Him up! I want a breeze in My flag. So I kiss Him. I wake Him up with My kisses."

The Shakti and Her Shiva laced Their fingers over me. I felt so safe that I wiggled.

"Oh, how You wake Me, My Queen," said the Shiva.

"I wake Him for the dance," said the Shakti. "And how You dance, My Lord! Oh! You can dance!"

I turned my face up to the Shakti's. Her eyes looking over me to Her Shiva were melting.

I saw the Shiva's mouth and eyes, too, soft and wet. He turned His head down to mine and drew His finger across my forehead. "You can imagine the dance," He said.

I felt a knowing, an excitement. Oh, I could imagine that dance! Shiva turns His wrists and buildings hoist to the sky. Shiva's foot arches and lovers cling. His knees unfold and with His leap monies glitter through the chutes of the marketplace. With the undulation of His back could come war and pestilence; His chest might ripple and a library rise and fall. The skin of His cheek might stretch taut and the new year's crop burst with fruit. At the flicker of His tongue, the dying hold the living; at the flinging of His arms, the quake erases a nation.

Like a drop of His sweat, my life might roll like a cat in the sun, purring, then springing after its prey. In a race down His side, my life could realize its promise. Caught in the crease of

130

His elbow, it might lie still. One day it would evaporate into the air He would breathe again.

I felt the knowing, the excitement. Oh, yes, I could imagine this dance!

The Shakti and Her Shiva curled Their arms about me in the nest of Their heat. The lips of the Shakti were reddened and full.

"Your limbs and Your contours!" said the Shakti to the Shiva. "You are like a melody."

"And You the breath that sings Me, Beloved," said the Shiva.

The room muted around me. And I slept again. But this time I dreamed. The shapes of the Queen and Her Lord were subtle now. They faded in and out. First She was enormous and the Shiva but Her finger's width. Then They were fighting. Could it be? They spoke harshly, and I could not see Her face. Then He chased, frantic and alone. Now She appeared again, like the Mother to the child crying after the nightmare. Now Her face is one of ecstasy: She collects to Her throbbing triangle of life His magnificent flowering tree of desire. Oh! How the picture blazed and faded in that dark and fiery place!

I was spinning then. Turning past the velvet and the tigers, into the floating peace of nothing and then the *aum* sound all around me. Past the mud and the roots, up between the fan of the lotus and over the castle entwined with roses and the long green rice. I sifted through the spiral of calves and peacocks, past the jeweled elephants and the curtains of principles and politics. Back through the rain and the sun and the wind.

I am back with you now, my daughter, my brother. I am back with you now, my lover, my friend. Back from the center of delight and pain. Up from the shades of death and the elixir of immortality. Up from the everlasting temple of the Shakti and Her Shiva. Up from the center of my heart and the secret of the world.

Mary
Queen of Heaven
(European)

Introduction

The Queen of Heaven in the person of Mary has been so manhandled that revulsion and pain have often outweighed my ability to connect with Her as Goddess. Indeed, through the ages, male church leaders have wrestled to stuff the love for the Mother they could not rid from their congregations into the box of Virgin Mother, shutting from common cultural understanding the sacredness of sexuality. Arguments about Her "history" have raged: church fathers have periodically attempted to prove Her neither divine nor maternal. But in the first centuries of the church's existence, leaders saw that without the worship of this combined Stella Maris, Juno and Mariamne, Ancient Spinner of Fate, and Begetter of Savior, their institution was doomed. Gothic cathedrals were regularly built over shrines to the Ancient Goddess and dedicated to "Our Lady," or Notre Dame, becoming truly palaces for the Queen of Heaven. Ambivalence born of denial and ignorance continues to this day: recently a Jesuit priest enthusiastically touted the inspiring new theory that Mary was really the first disciple of Christ. In agreeing to birth him, She became his first follower, goes this almost pitiful attempt to give the Great Originator the status of "first."

Like most people in modern culture, my first experience with the Goddess, unbeknownst to me, was with Mary. Raised as a Protestant rather than a Catholic, I met Her when I was seventeen in Mexico in the purple velvet, candlelit churches of Sinaloa. The sensuality and warmth of those rooms greatly comforted me; after the sparse, ascetic sanctuaries of my childhood in which the Spirit was the bodiless Word, these female-filled chapels washed me with relief.

I recently called on Mary at an afternoon mass in the Catholic church near the graveyard of my Protestant ancestors in southwest Ireland. While the elderly congregation chanted, "Hail, Mary, full of grace, the Lord is with Thee; Blessed art Thou among women and blessed is the fruit of Thy womb, Jesus; Holy Mary, Mother of God, pray for us sinners now, and at the hour of our deaths," I too softly chanted a prayer to the Star Goddess, borrowed from the traditional one that encodes Her own words: "Hail, Mary, full of grace, the dust of Whose feet are the hosts of Heaven; You are the white Moon among the stars and the desire of human hearts; You are the mystery: that if that which we seek we find not within, we will never find it without; For You were here at the beginning and You are that which is attained at the end of desire."

Challenged by friends to write the Christmas story from Mary's point of view, I came to terms with Her story as an extension of both the ancient story of Mayahuel and Her Fish Son and the Roman story of Juno Lucina as the yearly Creator of Light (see stories). My inspiration for Mary's story comes from the famous *Vierge Ouvrante*, a statue depicting the familiar, gentle Madonna and Child, whose opened hinges reveal inside Her: God, Jesus, the angels, and the saints of Heaven.

Mary and the Birth of Light

N THE MIDST
of the darkness, Mary, Queen of Heaven, opened the flower at
Her center. Gently, slowly, in the midst of the darkness, She
opened Herself, breathing a sugar of stars into the silent night.
Softly, tenderly, She spread the brown petals under the tips of
Her gathering hands. In the midst of the night, in the glitter of
stars, Mary dreamed and touched Her flower moist in the darkness.

In the midst of the darkness, the flower of Mary heated and
swelled. In the starry, breathing night, the fingers of Mary grew
firm and sure and the flower's edges melted into the center. Into
circles it melted, and out of the center came a cave in the shape
of a stable: a box of warm breathing in the midst of the night.
Out of Herself, to surround Her, birthed the Queen of Heaven
a cave: simple, humble, thick smelling, dark, and deep under
the night of the sky.

134

In the midst of the darkness, Mary's hands cradled Her flower. In the midst of the night, the cave cradled its Queen. In the midst of the cradle, in the midst of the circles, in the midst of the gathering, Her breath became music. Out of the music, out of the scent, out of the body of the Queen of Heaven came the animals of magic. Out of the breathing, out of the waves, out of the pliable, bending night came the animals that filled Her cave with their heat and their help.

Out of Mary's knees came the donkey. Shaggy, brown, carrier of burden, keeper of patience. Out of the knees of the Queen came the donkey, filling the cave with intractable certainty.

Out of the breasts of the Queen came the cow. White and red, milk and blood: cycles of pondering; enduring; full, placid heat in the stable of holiness.

Out of the feet of the Queen came the sheep. Simple and following, bleating their needs.

And when the music of holiness touched the rafters of the stable, the dove and its mate flew from Her arched back throat.

There in the dark, there in the shuffling heat, there in the cave song of the Queen of Heaven, there made the animals the nest for the light to come.

Then from the eyes of the Queen of Heaven rose up the beloved husband. Husband with the long hard back. Husband with the kissing hands. Husband to lie with, searching, rejoicing. Husband to enwrap and to touch again the flower at Her center. To have and to hold, the Queen of Heaven birthed the beloved husband.

Then, out of the swelling, out of the thick, heavy, coiling dark, out of the belly of the Queen of Heaven, out of Her, slipping and searing, into the soothing of the beloved husband, into the dark of the stable, into the giant night, slid the Sun of the World.

Out of the body of Mary came the Son of Light. There at Her breast He slept, while the beloved husband smoothed back the Queen of Heaven's hair. There slept the Child, filling the stable with light. There moved the animals. There slipped the tears down the face of the Queen. There in the night glowed the new light of the world, precious, whole, and alive at the center.

And it came to pass that the night was filled with multitudes of heavenly hosts praising Her name and crying hosannah to the highest and the lowest and all the bleating, mewing worlds that lay between.

Surrender

I hate the word *surrender*. It reminds me of war and rape and invisibility. Surrender has been a God word for me: it has been about having to buckle to the very thing I loathe in order to prove my piety. It has been about conquering myself, about strangling the full range of my emotion. In the attitude of surrender, I have been sure that my will, my innermost person, would lie squirming beneath a ruthless boot.

Needless to say, I have not wanted to surrender to anything or anybody. Indeed, I have spent most of my life identifying with my will and avoiding any activity I thought smacked of the loss of it. Certainly surrender could have nothing to do with my relationship to my juicy, flowing Goddess.

Or so I thought. It is true that my new understanding of surrender in Goddess consciousness does not degrade me or strip me of my sovereignty. I have been greatly healed, for example, by coming to know a legacy of witch women who, before they were burned for it, practiced a religion in which they bent, not to outside authority, but rather their own wills when they worked their craft. How sweet it has been to learn of civilizations that worshiped submission only to the womb and the tomb, not of one person to another.

But it is not true that my relationship to the Goddess has nothing to do with surrender. On the contrary, my sanity and sobriety depend on my admitting my powerlessness relative to Her Great Power, which I am not equipped to fully understand. The Order That I Cannot Know, I call Her. She embodies the facts as they are: in relationship to the Goddess, I must relinquish my childhood-based certainty that I can and must somehow force the facts to be different.

Refusing to surrender forced me to manipulate my perception of the facts. The world was too complicated if I did not simplify and call facts either black or white. I became obsessive about my efforts to change people, things, and even places in order to fit my version of how things should be. My attitudes, in turn, were manipulated by my obsessions. I was anxious and unreasonable without knowing it.

Surrender to the Power greater than myself has been the key to serenity. Paradoxically, when I live with ambiguity and helplessness, in the context of the Order That I Cannot Know, I gain a clarity and peace about my actions that I never had when I poured all my energy into trying to order my world. The Goddess is gray: She mirrors the states of a world in which everything, including myself, is constantly fluttering out of the reach of my butterfly net and silver pins. The truth is that I love and hate inconveniently; I get tired when I'm supposed to be performing; friends have feelings that dash my expectations; and my behavior disappoints others when it pleases me. I get angry; I get sick; grief does not clear up like a cold.

I became tremendously caught up in my efforts not to surrender. I created in my own life a personal control culture. I disregarded real information about myself and the world if it did not fit how I thought it should be. I became so unaware and unaccepting of my own feeling states that I could not imagine believing that my own real needs and wants might be the beginning of a conversation between myself and a Greater Power.

Today, Earth-centered spirituality has given me back the night, the dark, blood, Crone, under, and lower. It has given me back surrender, too. Earth-centered spirituality focuses on the truths—however murky and contradictory—of my body, partnership, and the Planet. Today, I can say that I picture surrender not as a rape or an invisibility, but as the awe I feel when I allow myself to accept—not fix or dominate—the endlessly shifting facts of existence.

Devi (DEE-vie)
Queen of All
(India)

Introduction

Devi, Sanskrit for "glowing with brilliant illumination" and cognate for the English word *divine*, is Goddess of All the Patterns of the Universe. She is not external or separate from Earth: She is the spiritual essence in all things that exist and occur.

The Harappans who first worshiped Her in India's Indus Valley called Her Danu, the same name used by the Celtic peoples of Ireland for their Mother. The Harappans were practicing agriculture by 5000 B.C.E. and by 3000 B.C.E. had built large cities of two-story brick buildings. The people of the Indian Danu flourished for another thousand years before the Aryan invaders arrived in 2000 B.C.E. The Vedas, the earliest writings of the conquerors, describe the massacre and enslavement of the Goddess worshipers by the Aryans, who enforced a caste system that subjugated dark-skinned peoples in the name of their holy male trinity: Indra, Mitra, and Varuna. Indra, the

Vedic story goes, killed Danu, and patriarchy replaced matri-focal, Earth-centered social systems.

Not for fifteen hundred years did the story of the Great Mother reemerge. In 500 C.E., storytellers from non-Aryan groups who had lived only at the fringes of Brahmanic caste influence put together the Tantras and the Puranas, new collections that painted the Goddess once again as powerful, She Who could obliterate the entire universe by closing Her eyes even for a second.

Devi, they called Her, the ultimate Shakti, the One Whose image all other names and forms illuminate. Splitting the Goddess into multiple aspects may have been a demotion in many cultures; the very same act, however, has also served to focus and clarify Her immense complexity. As separate chapters in an epic story teach a whole worldview, so separate personifications of the Great Mother can paradoxically instruct about Her simplicity. Knowing Her as Devi, Shakti, Maya, and Kali (see stories) and by Her hundreds of other names and forms emboldens and humbles us at once.

The areas least affected by Brahmanic Aryan influence in today's India are the Malabar coast of the southwest and Bengal and Assam of the northeast. Malabar remains largely matrilineal and matrifocal, and the practice of polyandry (one woman having several husbands) was common until the last century. Worship of the Ammas—the Mothers—is of primary concern there, and numerous woman poets over the centuries have thrived, more than one writing joyously of lesbian love. Tantric orders in Bengal and Assam include women in the highest clergy possible, and caste discrimination is discouraged.

I adapted Devi's traditional story from the one told in Merlin Stone's *Ancient Mirrors of Womanhood*. This story, in turn, was drawn from several books of the Puranas. I have used a crown and a purple cloth to invoke Her great power and centeredness in my life.

Devi and the Battle with Durga the Evil One

NCE, LONG AGO in the heavens over the land of India, Durga the Evil One took the shape of a Demon Buffalo, raised up on his hind legs, and drove the Gods and Goddesses from Heaven, forcing them to seek refuge in the forests of Earth. Bellowing, he smashed the holy places and crashed through the skies to the Earth below.

There Durga the Evil One stole fires from hearths, pushed great rivers from their paths, and dried up the rains. He uprooted mountains with his horns and dusted himself with the powder of gold and copper he found there.

The people cried out to the God Shiva. "Dancing Prince! Save us from the monster Durga. Muscle the Evil One away. Tear out his horns!"

Prince Shiva was powerful, but he found the strength of his armies no match for the Durga. The Demon Buffalo continued his rampage.

Then the people gathered at the palace of the God Kalatri. "Guardian of the Night," they called out. "Sneak up on the Durga. Tear out his tail from behind, and when he whirls to meet you, kill him with your power. We beg you. We are longing to be safe."

But Kalatri, too, found that his powers were nothing against the Evil One's storm. So the people gathered their jewels and went to the Devi. Into the circle of Her throne room they flooded and fell on their faces before Her.

Devi sat at the center on a throne, half of which was made of fire and the other half of water. A tree grew high on either side of Her, and the scent of lotus hung in the air. Green threads sprayed out from Her thousand hands, and Devi's three eyes glowed—one black, one white, and one the color of blood.

"Great One!" the people rumbled. "Luminous Mother! You of the thousand arms. Queen of Earth, Queen of Fire, Queen of Water, Queen of Air. You Who hold the threads of all matter in Your hands!

"Neither Shakti nor Kalatri can leash the mighty Durga. We need You, O Great One. Put Your sword in his heart."

Devi the Great One rode to meet Durga on Her lion. The Demon Buffalo had created soldiers beyond number for this battle. He also had 120 million chariots and 120 million horses. With a whoop of rage, the Evil One hailed a storm of arrows on Devi, but they fell from Her body like raindrops.

Then the Demon blew hurricanes with his breath. He tore boulders off mountains and uprooted trees. He hurled the trees and rocks at Devi, but they touched Her like sand might touch a cliff in a breeze. Then the Evil One lashed a huge wave from the ocean with his tail and sent it to drown Devi's lion.

Though Devi's arms were busy with many battles, She was angered at the attack on Her lion. She took a mighty rope and lassoed Durga's tail. At that instant, Durga the Buffalo became Durga the Lion. Devi plunged Her sword through the Lion, but Durga the Lion then turned into Durga the Man, sword and shield in his hands. When Devi slung Her spear at Durga the Man, Durga became Durga the Elephant.

And so it was that the Evil One kept changing forms and creating more and more evil. No one lost and no one won. A mountain of evil grew up, and Devi sliced it into seven smaller hills.

Finally Durga showed himself in his true form. The Demon Buffalo stepped into battle without a disguise. This time he was Durga the Evil One, and he too had one thousand arms.

Then came the battle. One thousand arms of Durga flew against one thousand arms of Devi. Suddenly, just when it seemed that the clanging and cutting and searing could get no hotter, Devi stopped.

She pulled in Her one thousand arms and sat Herself down and was silent. Then slowly She spread a purple cloth before Her and began to eat and drink of the fruits and wine that appeared there. Devi chewed and swallowed with pleasure, and Her three eyes shone.

The whole world watched. People held their breaths. Why had Devi stopped fighting? Was She admitting defeat?

Then Devi stood. When She called to the Evil One, Her voice sounded like cymbals and bells. "Durga! Laugh your last laugh!" She said. Durga roared. Devi leapt up and set Her foot on his neck. Then with Her thousand arms, She tore the thousand arms of the Evil One from his body. Then She braided his arms into Her hair until they rose up like a crown about Her face.

The people cheered. "We are saved! Victory! Queen of the World! Savior! Devi!" they shouted, waving branches and singing.

From that day forth, Devi was called Devi the Luminous by Her people. But they also called Her Durga, for at the battle of the Buffalo Demon they saw Durga become a part of the Devi.

Sun Woman

(Australia)

Introduction

Before the European Caucasians began to force themselves onto the continent of Australia two centuries ago, the aboriginals, who prefer to be called Australoids, were the land's original peoples. Then they numbered five hundred tribes and three hundred thousand individuals. Today they are only forty thousand and have been largely pushed out of the fertile eastern sections of the continent onto the deserts of the central regions.

The Australoid peoples tell the stories of the Ancients who lived under the world and came out at the beginning to sing into being the rivers, the ranges, the salt pan, and the sand dunes. The ancients wrapped the world in a web of song, a net of music trails that even today enliven the land's forms and inhabitants, though the colonizer may be deaf to the sacred sound. Their song sung, the Ancients went back to the cave holes that bore Them, leaving the records of these wondrous cantatas on wooden and stone *churingas* (record sticks) for the people, to be guarded by every generation forevermore.

Yhi is the Sun Woman of the Arunta people who now live just west of Queensland in central Australia. She is the Goddess who grows both old and young as the year changes (like Changing Woman of the Navajo: see story). Every day She reenters the Womb of Life under the sand where all the Ancient Spirits live. Sun Woman, like Amaterasu Omikami of Japan (see story), Allat of ancient Arabia, and Sun Goddesses of Argentinians, Inuit (Eskimo) peoples, and ancient Anatolians, defies the stereotype that Sun deities are always male.

I borrowed the seed of Merlin Stone's tale in *Ancient Mirrors of Womanhood* to write Sun Woman's story, which honors the Twelve-Step program concept of "one day at a time" that is so helpful in my life. I invoke Sun Woman with that slogan and have also carried a bit of red cloth and a wood chip to remind me of Her.

The Tasks for Each Day

EEP DOWN UNDER
the sands of the desert live all the Spirits who have died or have
not yet been born. All day long the Spirit People sew a huge red
dress, needles flashing in and out, working seams and hems so
the dress will fit just right.

The dress is for Sun Woman. Every night Sun Woman
returns to the Spirit People under the sand and slips into the
new dress They've prepared for Her. Then, just before every
dawn, the Spirit People give Sun Woman a huge log, which
They light for Her journey up to the Earth People.

Each night, the Spirit People make just one dress and ready
just one log for one torch. That one dress and torch are what
Sun Woman takes for Her trip across the sky every day.

It wasn't always like that, though. About a thousand years
after time began, the Spirit People began to complain. "We're
tired of making a dress every night," They said. "Sun Woman

won't mind if We make a hundred dresses and pile them up. That way We can take a vacation. We can stack up lots of logs for Her torches, too."

It was summertime then, and Sun Woman was old. It took Her a long time to cross the sky. That evening when She hobbled under the desert sands for the night, the Spirit People gathered about Her. "Sun Woman, Sun Woman," They said. "We're tired of sewing every night. It's the same thing over and over again. Sun Woman, We want to work very hard for a while and pile up a lot of dresses and logs, and then We want to rest."

Sun Woman surprised the Spirit People with Her answer. "I'm tired too," She said. She let out a big sigh and sat down heavily. "I'm exhausted. Forget about making dresses and getting torches," She said. "I'm too tired to go up to the Earth People for a while."

The Spirit People looked at each other. "But, Sun Woman," They said, "if You don't go up there, there won't be any daytime."

Sun Woman shrugged. "If You can take a vacation, so can I," She said.

The Spirit People looked at each other again. Then an Old Woman Spirit spoke out, "I know about being tired, Sun Woman," She said. "I lived a very long time among the Earth People. My life there was very hard. But every morning, Sun Woman, You came again out of the ground, and there before me was a new day. I needed You, Sun Woman. I needed Your light so I could keep on."

Then an Old Man Spirit began to speak. "I lost my wife and children when I was a young man," He said. " 'I cannot face my life without my family,' I said. 'I want to die.' But my friend came and held my hands. 'Don't face all the days of your life,' my friend said. 'Just face today. See. Here comes Sun Woman. Just stay this one day, until She leaves us tonight.' " The Old Man Spirit stopped for a moment. Then He said, "That's what I did. I stayed just for one day. And I kept doing that. Just staying for one day each day. That's how I lived for a long time—one day at a time."

"Sun Woman," said a Baby Spirit. "If You don't make Your journey every day, I don't want to be born."

The Spirit People nodded and talked aloud together. "The Earth People need Sun Woman. And Sun Woman needs Us," They said. Sun Woman soaked Her feet as She listened.

That night the Spirit People and Sun Woman agreed that no one would take a vacation. The Spirit People would ready one dress and one log for each of Sun Woman's journeys. And Sun Woman would travel up to the Earth People and cross their sky every day.

That's how it's been ever since. Sometimes Sun Woman is young, and then She hurries across the sky. Sometimes She is old, and then She walks very slowly. But always She comes, and always She returns to the land under the desert sands where the Spirit People busy Themselves with the one red dress and one burning log for each day.

Cerridwen (SAIR-i-dwen)
Queen of Wisdom
(Ireland)

Introduction

The Celtic people, called the Gauls by the Romans, once populated lands extending from the mouth of the Danube in Romania to the western coast of France. Called Galatians in ancient Poland and Spain, they were also the Galatians of ancient Turkey, to whom the Christian Paul wrote the missionary letter of the New Testament. In a saga that mirrors that of Earth-revering peoples today, this many-tribed and -languaged group fled continually from Roman, Teuton, Angle, Saxon, and Jute invaders until they finally came to occupy only the outskirts of their once tremendous territory: today's Ireland, Scotland, Wales, Cornwall, and Brittany. Settled in this island world, they received the gift of writing from the Goddess Bridget (see story) and began to record their oral traditions.

In the context of legends that remember women as governmental, martial, political, and oracular leaders, Celtic storytellers told of Cerridwen, who personified the religious mystery central to the Celts: reincarnation within the Womb of the Goddess. Cerridwen's name means "Cauldron of Wisdom," the vessel of disintegration and rebirth, a concept that celebrates the cyclical rather than linear nature of time. The Cauldron, paralleling the Christian cross or sword, is a pivotal symbol for Goddess worshipers the world over. It is called by Hindus the Pot of Blood in Kali's Hand (see story of Kali), and by Egyptians the Underworld Womb or Lake of Fire. (The latter concept was borrowed by Christian storytellers for their diabolized Underworld hell.) The Cauldron is the precursor to the Christian Holy Grail or the mythological chalice of Christ's last supper. The Celts said that the endlessly boiling Cauldron was stirred by Nine Sisters (see Bridget's story). The Nine Sisters represent the Holy Trinity of Maiden, Mother, and Crone, each able to manifest all three of Her selves. They are related to both the Nine Muses of Greek mythology and Chinese stories in which the Great Goddess was represented by Nine Tripod Mixing Vessels.

The Cauldron's magic, like that of the Goddess Herself, is that of endlessly shifting shapes. Shamanic initiations in many cultures include hallucinatory experiences of psychic dismemberment, boiling, and rebirth in the Pot of the World (see stories of Inanna and Ereshkigal, Sedna, and Isis). The "year and a day" required for initiation in Celtic mythology (a time span encoded in dozens of today's fairy tales) refers to the thirteen 28-day lunar months of a year with one more day to make 365 days.

Cerridwen, as the Dark Aspect of the Triple Goddess, also took the form for the Celts of the sacred Sow. In this form, She symbolized Earth, Giver of Life and Death. In an excellent example of cross-cultural symbolism, Cerridwen shared Her Pig shape with the Goddesses Freya, Demeter, and Astarte (see stories). Ancient peoples in Spain and Malta, as well, worshiped the Goddess as Mother Pig in sacred rites.

I invented Cerridwen's story, basing it on the one told by Merlin Stone in *Ancient Mirrors of Womanhood*. That story, in turn, was put together from the sixteenth-century work of the

Welsh Elis Grufydd, who collected and recorded verbal accounts of ancient beliefs. Cerridwen, for me, is a mixture of Inanna and Ereshkigal; Her transformative powers parallel those of Isis. But I call on Cerridwen when the concern at hand is socially shocking or horrifying. To invoke Her, I make a fire of herbs or rubbing alcohol in a small, lidded, iron Cauldron.

The Cauldron of Magic
and Regeneration

T THE BEGIN-
ning, Cerridwen, Queen of Wisdom, took the form of a huge
bird and swallowed a piece of the sky. When, afterward, She
felt life stir in Her, She flew to the mountain where the Nine
Sisters live. There, with the Sisters moaning and shuddering
about Her, She took the form of Woman among Them and
began to swell with life. Truly then She was wondrous to behold: eyes blue as the day sky, skin black as the night sky, and
hair the color of the sun.

And so it was that Cerridwen, Queen of Wisdom, made
Her home on the mountain of the Nine Sisters—Three forever
young, Three forever in the middle of life, and Three forever old.

Cerridwen's child was born under the light of a star. When
Her own moaning finally ceased and She held the boy bloody
in Her arms, She washed him clean with Her tears and sang

him a thousand little songs. Like his Mother, the boy's skin was black as night and his hair as hard to look at as the sun. But instead of day-sky eyes, the boy's eyes were brown like the wings of his Mother when She'd conceived him.

Cerridwen named the boy Morfran. She saw how curious he was; how his tiny fingers explored every stone and flower in his little world. She knew that someday She wanted him to drink from the Cauldron of the Deep, from which all things come and to which all things return. With the Nine Sisters, She resolved to ready him for that day when he would drink from the source of Her wisdom.

And so, as Morfran grew, his needs and his wishes were respected. Morfran thus grew to respect himself, the mountain, Cerridwen, and the Nine Sisters, who together formed the fabric of his life.

Cerridwen taught Morfran the names and properties of every herb and root that grew on the mountain. She showed him the precise movements of the sun, the moon, and all the stars.

The day came when Cerridwen knew that Her plan for Her son could be realized. She saw that he honored himself, his mountain, and his family. She marked just thirteen moons from Morfran's thirteenth year. Then would be the time for him to drink from the Cauldron of the Deep; then he would be filled with the power and magic of Her wisdom.

Onto the fire tended by the Nine Sisters, Cerridwen and Morfran swung the huge black pot. Into it they dropped herbs and roots, each picked at the proper moment of the planets and the stars. They added the foam of inspiration and prophecy from the faraway sea and the ability to change shape from the clouds in the sky.

Cerridwen chanted this chant as they readied the Cauldron:

> *That you know what you know*
> *And see what you see:*
> *This is the brew we'll brew for thee.*
> *In My Cauldron Deep we'll brew this brew*
> *That wisdom walk far when it walk with you.*

The brew would be stirred for a year and a day, and then Morfran would taste of its first three magic drops.

One day, as Morfran sat resting from stirring the brew, he was startled to see someone very like himself appear on the other side of the billowing smoke. This stranger was clearly a boy, but he was larger than Morfran, with skin so pale that purplish blue marks showed on it. The new boy drew back when he saw Morfran and covered his eyes against the brightness of Morfran's hair.

"Who are you?" asked Morfran.

"Gwion," said the boy.

"Where do you come from?" asked Morfran.

"The valley," said the boy.

"Who is your Mother?" asked Morfran.

The boy said nothing. Then he tried to look at Morfran. "I can't look at your head," he said. "Your hair's like the sun."

"It's my Mother's hair," said Morfran. "Hey, I know." Morfran scooped up some ash from the fire and rubbed it on his hair. The brightness immediately dulled. "Look now," said Morfran.

The boy looked. This time he could keep his eyes on Morfran. Morfran could see that the boy looked frightened and hungry. When he handed him a bowl of food, the boy flinched but then grabbed it and ate quickly.

"Who is your Mother?" asked Morfran again when Gwion had finished eating.

"My mother is the richest, nicest queen in the world, and my father is the strongest, most wonderful king," he said.

That evening Cerridwen tied a cloth around Her head so Gwion could look at Her. Cerridwen, the Nine Sisters, and Morfran shared their food and made a bed for Gwion, and they listened as he boasted about how powerful and good his parents were. When Cerridwen asked him why he'd left his parents, Gwion said he was tired and went to bed.

Cerridwen and Morfran sat together a long time in the dark. "Mother," said Morfran finally. "Gwion is not well, and he is lying about his parents."

"What a magician you're going to be," said Cerridwen, "when you are so wise already."

The next day Cerridwen asked Gwion how he'd gotten the bruises on his arms and legs. Gwion began to cry. The Nine Sisters held him, and after a long time Gwion told them that his parents were not really a king and a queen. They beat him, he said, and sometimes he thought they did not even know his name. His job was to fetch things for his parents, and even when he did that, they hit him anyway.

"You are welcome here on the mountain," said Cerridwen.

So Gwion stayed. He found that he'd come to the mountain of Cerridwen, Queen of Wisdom, and that Her son Morfran was stirring the Cauldron of the Deep, from which all things come and to which all things return. In less than a year and a day now, Gwion learned, Morfran would drink the first three drops of the Cauldron's brew and would walk in wisdom and magic. Gwion was amazed at all that he saw. He had never felt so free and safe and cared for. Many times he pretended that his real mother was Cerridwen and that Morfran was not his friend but his brother. But many other times, Gwion was scared. He remembered so clearly his pain and loneliness in the valley, and he was sure it had all happened because he was bad. In his secret heart, Gwion began to hate Morfran. Even though he helped Morfran stir the brew, played games with him at the side of the fire, and told stories with him at night, he cringed to see Morfran getting hugged by Cerridwen, and he told himself that Morfran was ugly and weak.

As the year and a day drew to a close, Gwion began to ask himself why it should be Morfran who got to drink the first three drops from the Cauldron of the Deep. "He has everything," said Gwion to himself. "Why should he get those drops, instead of me?"

As the brew neared its time, it grew thicker and harder to stir. On the night before Morfran was to turn thirteen, Cerridwen stirred the Cauldron the whole night long. In the morning, Morfran took Her place. "Soon, son," said Cerridwen. She smiled at him, and Her blue eyes shone with pride.

Gwion wished he had a mother who would look at him like that. Today, he even felt how much he liked Morfran. "But it's not fair," he told himself. Then Gwion tensed. He saw that Cerridwen had gone away to lie down. He looked anxiously at Morfran. Morfran was looking into the fire, his face calm but his eyes glowing.

Then Gwion saw that Cerridwen had fallen asleep.

"It's ready, Gwion," said Morfran softly.

Something burst inside of Gwion. He ran at Morfran and shoved him away as hard as he could. Then three times he dipped the tip of his own finger into the huge pot. When he'd tasted the last drop, the Cauldron split in two with a roar. The liquid inside smothered the fire underneath and poured out all over the ground.

Morfran shouted. Cerridwen awoke from Her nap. With a cry of rage, She tore the cloth from Her fiery hair and lunged after Gwion.

Terrified, Gwion used the magic now inside him to turn himself into a rabbit. He leapt away, and Cerridwen turned Herself into a greyhound and bounded after him. Just as She was about to catch him, Gwion changed to a fish and plunged into a river. Cerridwen's body took the shape of an otter and dove at the tail of the fish. Nearly out of strength, Gwion turned himself into a bird and shuddered to see that Cerridwen was now a giant hawk gaining on him with every push of Her wings.

Exhausted now, Gwion spied, in the valley from which he'd come, a pile of wheat. There he plummeted and turned himself into a tiny piece of grain.

Cerridwen turned Herself then into a black-crested hen in that yard with the pile of wheat, and she pecked and pecked until She'd eaten the boy whole.

Then, for a second time, Cerridwen the Bird felt life growing in Her. But this time, when She went to the mountain with the Nine Sisters, Her son was there, and Cerridwen had rage in Her heart. This child inside Her had taken from Her son what was rightfully his. She swore She would never let this boy inside Her live. She waited out the birth, knowing She would kill him when he was born.

But when the baby came and She held it bloody in Her arms, She could not bear to kill it.

No one knows what happened to Gwion. Some say Gwion got his wish and that Cerridwen Herself raised him as Her second son. Others say that he was raised in the valley from where he'd come, but this time by parents who could respect and love him. Those people say he became a great poet and magician who could change his shape at will and tell the future.

The Nine Sisters, it is said, pieced together the Cauldron of the Deep, and on the mountain They stir it still, keepers of the place from which all things come and to which all things return.

And Morfran? No one knows either what became of him. But many say he walks the Earth still, with hairs gray from the ashes he applied so long ago. He is not a poet or a magician, people say, but a wise man who knows what he knows and sees what he sees.

Maya (MY-yuh)
Masked Woman of the Primordial Void
(India)

Introduction

The Goddess Maya of India is the relentless Process of Life itself. The spell of Maya is blind life energy continuously manifesting itself: originating, growing, decaying, and vanishing, forever veiling from Her creatures the true nature of Her Void. Maya is the neutral screen on which the endless characters and plots of our souls' moving pictures project and complete their dramas. She is the inward dream of the senses and the cosmic mystery, mixing the desire of human hearts and supernatural tension in a paradox of wisdom and enchantment. In Maya, there is nothing static, nothing abiding. Demonic and beneficent, She is the name of our illusion and delusion: Her face both beguiles and opens the way to transcendent enlightenment.

Hindu mythology dresses the Mystery of the World in fantastic personifications. Maya, like the Shakti, Kali (a form of the Shakti), and Devi (see stories), are all manifestations of the

160

primordial Feminine in Whose embrace the great Masculine energies of Brahma, Vishnu, and Shiva come to throbbing, proliferating, and perishing life. Although most renditions of Hindu mythologies suffer from the pervasiveness of patriarchal bias, today's actual worship of the Great Feminine in India is explicit and inspiringly current.

Maya's name is shared by Goddesses of Mystery and Illusion in many parts of the world. Central Americans called Her Mayahuel (see story); the Greeks called Her Maia; the Irish, Maga; and the Scandinavians, Maj.

Maya's story has something of the flavor of a Zen koan and is a retelling of the traditional one recounted by Heinrich Zimmer in *Myths and Symbols in Indian Art and Culture*. The movie *Cinema Paradiso* was a brilliant evocation of Maya for me. I think of Her when I play with a kaleidoscope; this Goddess helps me come to terms with both my need to make the universe meaningful and my sometimes overwhelming sense of its meaninglessness.

The Goddess Behind the God

IT HAPPENED that the saint Narada had practiced so long and thoroughly the renunciation of the things of the earthly plane that the God Vishnu Himself went walking with him. The two talked deeply about many things. But the God Vishnu only smiled enigmatically and was silent when Narada asked that he be allowed to know the great Vishnu's Maya.

Narada insisted, however, and said, "Great Vishnu, I know that You Yourself are only a manifestation of Your Maya. If I am to truly know You, My Lord, I must know the Goddess from Whom You come."

Vishnu curved His beautiful lips and told Narada that He recommended the contentment that came with their own friendship. He said that knowledge of the Maya was too much of an undertaking, even for such a one as the saint Narada.

Narada was silent awhile as he and Vishnu strolled in the sheltered hermit's grove. Though they talked of other things, it happened that Narada persisted in his plea to know the real power of the God, and Vishnu finally shrugged and relented.

He took Narada to a place on the desert where the heat shimmered in the sands and the white ball of the sun seemed to scorch the very blood. Narada's thirst grew, but he rested in the knowledge that soon he would know the Maya of the world.

"Narada, I am thirsty," said Vishnu finally. He pointed in the direction of a tiny hamlet of houses moving in and out of their vision like waves in the light. "Pray go to the first house and bring Me a glass of water."

Narada bowed and made his way across the burning hills to the first house. He knocked.

When the door opened, a young woman greeted Narada and bade him enter, gazing at him all the while with eyes that filled Narada suddenly and completely with mysterious feeling. And it happened that the feeling so overtook Narada that he simply forgot why he had come.

His eyes with the woman's seemed to lock, and he continued to return to their depths as he drank from her dipper of water. How very like his Lord's they were! How kind and fathomless at once!

Soon Narada met her family in the next room. Her father and mother sat at a feast table, along with three brothers, all of whom had wives and beautiful children of various ages. Like the woman herself, none of the family commented on his arrival but seemed to accept him as if they'd known he was coming.

The foods of the evening were sumptuous, and Narada felt himself held in a sweetness of pleasure. It was a sensation— what with the delicacies and the eyes and conversation of this woman—like none he had ever known before.

It came to pass that there flowered between Narada and the woman a friendship that brought both peace and joy and an enthusiasm for the future. Before long, the two had wed, and all the village rejoiced.

Eleven years went by. Narada joined with the family of his wife in the seasonal tasks of farm and home. He and the woman had three children. Narada felt richness and gratitude overflow in his heart.

In the twelfth year, the rains came with a fury rarely seen before. Straw huts and cattle were carried away on their torrent, and people fled. One howling night, the waters began to flood the house. Narada woke his wife and their children, and, clinging to each other, the family made its way into the dark. Narada carried the smallest child and held tight to the hand of the next, who clutched her brother's hand in her own. The mother clung to the hand of the eldest. The current tore at their legs, and the parents could barely manage their burdens.

Narada made himself heard over the gale that they must find the top of the hill.

Suddenly, at the moment lightning cracked the sky, a mountain of water ripped Narada's baby from his arms. With a cry, he lunged after the child and lost the girl's hand. Another stroke of lightning revealed the avalanche of water that struck Narada's wife and children. Helpless, their screams piercing his heart, Narada saw his family sucked under the deep.

The next thing Narada knew, he was atop the hill of the village, able only to weep.

Narada then felt a hand on his shoulder. He looked to find the God Vishnu beside him, shaking his head gently. "You come at last," said the God. "I have been waiting for you almost half an hour. Do you now understand the secret of My Maya?"

VI

Goddess As Archetype

J ungians use the word *archetype* to talk about the blank molds of expectation with which we humans come into the world. No matter what the context or the age, all human cultures seem to hold ideal concepts of home, hero, healer, mother, father, or trickster. It is as if we humans are born with a row of labeled white plates on the mantelpieces of our minds. Depending on the culture we live in and the details of our environments, we then find sketched on our mother plate, for example, the specifics of what mother is in our case. Sometimes that plate takes our situation-specific inscription rather well: our sketch defies little of the promise of that archetypal plate. Often, though, our mother plate cracks or shatters under the weight of differences between the sketch of our particular mother and the expected mother plate with which we are born. The Jungians use this concept of the broken archetype to explain the tremendous pain we associate with lack of tender mothering by an actual mother, even if our caretaking experiences were themselves not extraordinarily painful.

In other words, even if we have not experienced loving mothering, we do know it on what Jungians call the archetypal level. We therefore experience great longing to unite with an actual life experience that matches what we know archetypally to be possible. Similarly, a person without a home aches after the sense of being home, even if she has never known a safe, private place of her own, even if the weather is fine.

For years now, women, people of color, and people with physical differences have wrestled to identify, remove, and replace the common images of ourselves that narrow our hopes and compel us to think of ourselves in life-deforming ways. Stories about the Goddess begin to glue together the archetype of the Great Feminine that has been shattered by the culture's stereotypes.

For, even if we choose not to worship the Goddess, we can find in Her stories images of our true inner and outer selves—many hued, endlessly costumed and shaped, awesome, loving, raging, tender, knowing, able, and proud. The Goddess changes our posture; no longer do *Great* and *Feminine* seem contradictions in terms. Like children with role models, our eyes melt in adoration of these ways we can copy, and we find ourselves growing—feet sure, stomachs round, and voices bold and free.

Mbaba Mwana Waresa
(mah-BAH-bah mah-WAH-nah wah-REH-sah)
Great Rain Mother of All

(Zulu People)

Introduction

The oldest human remains and the earliest human tools ever made have both been found on the continent of Africa, in today's Kenya and Tanzania. From this vast land, which stretches five thousand miles north to south and likewise east to west, come the human ancestors of early European culture and the Divine Ancestress Herself. In those beginning times, from 30,000 to 15,000 B.C.E., when politics and religion were one, nearly identical paintings that froze the sacred Life Spirits on the womb walls of caves have been found in ancient France and Spain, South Africa, Zimbabwe, Morocco, Libya, and around the Sahara Desert. As from the center of a great web, the peoples of Africa must have migrated over the millennia to the slender ends of their world. The bone characteristics of the skeletal remains of ancient Europeans show unmistakably their black African heritage.

Out of Africa, the cradle of a thousand human cultures, rises the Goddess by as many names. The Zulu people of Natal, South Africa, understood Her, like so many people the world over, as personifying the Water of Life. Other peoples worship Her in the river, the lake, and the ocean (see story of Yemaya and Iamanja). The Zulus call Her Mother of Rain, Mbaba Mwana Waresa.

Since the Zulu people are renowned for their beautiful and complicated dances for all sacred occasions, Her traditional story in this collection, adapted from the one told in *Ancient Mirrors of Womanhood*, may well enact a reverential dance for rain. The October sky actually sprinkled a couple of years ago during a Berkeley evening of telling Her story and chanting Her name. I dream of the day we take to the streets, en masse, with pots and pans in honor of Her water. Mbaba's story also pricks me with hope about our far-reaching abilities to take back the idea of beauty from the mongers of self-hatred.

The Choice of the Wise Husband

VER THE GREEN, brown, and blue Earth lives the Sky Mama. Ma-baba.

In the lightning and thunder hear Her voice and Her drums. Ma-wana.

The glistening, the slicking, the wa-wet drops slanting, sleeking down are Her arms and Her legs, Her hands and Her feet. Wa-resa.

Ma-baba Ma-wana Wa-resa.

In the rainbow is Her smile.

Mbaba Mwana Waresa.

Mbaba Mwana Waresa.

It is Mbaba Mwana Waresa who pours down Her sacred waters to Her thirsty people, plants, animals, lakes, and rivers. Mbaba Mwana Waresa cleans, cools, quenches, fills, soaks, pounds, drizzles, and streams. Mbaba Mwana Waresa, Rain Mother of All, is the One without Whom There Is No Life.

In Her absence we long for Her, dance for Her. Mbaba! we cry. Mwana! Waresa! Gone too long, we die, Mbaba. Come to us!

In Her presence we put away our fans. We are thankful. We collect Her sacred waters in our pots. We shiver and dream of fire. Mbaba! Mwana! Waresa! Your noise is mighty. The night is long. We want a fire and a story.

The fire is built. Here is the story.

Once upon a time Mbaba Mwana Waresa wished for a husband. When none of the Gods in Heaven pleased Her, She went to Earth to look for the wisest, most handsome man She could find. When the young man She had chosen heard tell he was to marry Mbaba Mwana Waresa, he went away by himself for a long while to think and prepare himself.

Mbaba Mwana Waresa returned to Heaven to ready Herself for the wedding. But to the astonishment of all in Heaven, Mbaba Mwana Waresa did nothing to decorate Herself. Instead She asked Her friend to dress as the Zulu bride. Wondering at Mbaba's request, Her friend had the finest clothes wrapped about her body and her hair braided into a hundred delicate plaits with beautiful beads laced at each end. Gold and silver bracelets were coiled at her wrists and ankles, and sacred dyes were painted on her cheeks and forehead. Great hoops were hung in her ears, and shining stones threaded on thin copper wires beneath her arms jingled softly as she moved. The womb shell of life was hung on her forehead.

When Mbaba Mwana Waresa saw that Her friend was ready, She did an even stranger thing. She removed all Her own precious beads and Her rainbow-colored robes. With a sharp stone She cut all the tiny beautiful curls from Her head. She smeared Her smooth black skin with pale gray ashes and wrapped Herself in the torn skin of a zebra.

Then Mbaba Mwana Waresa declared that the heavenly pair was ready to make the journey to the village where the young groom awaited Her.

The young man knew the wedding day had come when the sky above him darkened and lightning cracked across the clouds. He heard the beat of Her drums in the thunder that followed. The young man held his shoulders very straight as he went to stand in the rain of his good fortune.

The women from the village chosen as wedding attendants gathered with him, and when the Goddess and Her friend arrived, everyone bowed low in reverence. Then all watched to see if the young man would know which of the two from heaven was to be his Wife.

The young man did not hesitate. He extended his hands to Mbaba Mwana Waresa, knowing Her even in the torn skin of a zebra, body gray with ashes, and the hair of Her lovely head shaved away.

"Welcome, Mbaba Mwana Waresa," said the young man. "You need no precious beads, nor fine clothes, nor silver and gold jewelry to show me Who You are. For I see in Your eyes the richness of the Earth, the bounty of the harvest, and the power of Your thunder and lightning. How honored I am to be Your husband."

Mbaba Mwana Waresa smiled. She had chosen well, for this young man was wise enough to see the truth. The friend of Mbaba Mwana Waresa and all the attendants began to clap and sing. The wedding ceremony was held, and then Mbaba Mwana Waresa took Her husband back to Heaven, where he lives with Her to this very day. Mbaba Mwana Waresa.

Juno Lucina (JEW-no lu-CHEE-nah)
Queen of Light
(Italy)

Introduction

Like Freya of northern Europe and Isis of Egypt (see stories), Juno, the supreme Roman Goddess, was far too powerful to be fully subordinated by the patriarchy. Instead, Her glory persisted, and She took dozens of forms for Her worshipers. As Juno Fortuna, She was Mistress of Fate; as Regina, She reigned Queen of Heaven. As Juno Moneta, She gave us the word *money* and was the Great Adviser and Admonisher. Juno Februa was Goddess of Erotic Love; Juno Populonia was Mother of the People. As Juno Lucina, Queen of Celestial Light, She is related to Her Greek counterpart, Hera, from Whose breasts streamed the Milky Way.

The name *Juno* is cognate to the Etruscan *Uni*, root of the word *Universe*, and to *Yoni*, the name for the sacred Vulva and Womb of all life. Her lily, or lotus, universal symbol for the Yoni, enabled this Three-in-One Divine Mother to conceive the God Mars without the aid of Her consort Jupiter, and thus was conferred on Her the title of Blessed Virgin, borrowed by Christian storytellers for their Mary.

Every woman embodied a portion of the Great Juno in her "juno" or soul, corresponding to the "genius" in every man. Patriarchal vocabularies dropped the word *juno*, retaining and elevating the word *genius* and, lexicographically speaking, depriving women of their souls. Her sacred month was June, in which She oversaw marriages and family matters. June is believed to this day to be the luckiest month for weddings.

I have used olives, peacock feathers, and cowrie shells to invoke Juno. I wrote the story of Juno Lucina in order to conceptualize Her regenerative power as it relates to Her Son, the Sun or the Seasonal Year. The story personifies the processes of death and birth in the shifting of light from Fall Equinox to Winter Solstice. (See also stories of Isis, Demeter and Persephone, Inanna and Ereshkigal, Amaterasu Omikami, Changing Woman, and Sun Woman.)

Farewell to the Sun King

THE GODDESS Juno is very great and not easy to understand. For this reason, Her people give Her many names and tell many stories about Her. When the people watch the light of the Year turn short, then long again, they call Her Juno Lucina and tell the story of how She gives birth to Her Son, the Year, how He dies, and how He is born again from Great Mother Juno. Here is one of the stories they tell.

Juno Lucina sat very still at the table before the mirror at the darkest end of her cave. On the table lay a black box and a long dark vial and a comb in the shape of a serpent. Lucina was not looking in the glass at Her reflection, which, even with Her head bowed, gave out a violet and silver light. Juno Lucina, Queen of Light, was alone tonight, hands resting flat on the front of Her robes the color of pumpkins and dying leaves. She could feel the Baby stirring inside Her, and She felt the same wonder and knowing She felt every year. Soon the new Sun King would be born, and She was glad.

But Lucina's eyes, when She lifted them to study Her face, were sad. Tonight she must say good-bye to Her grown-up Sun King. She moved Her hands to the tabletop and stared into Her face. "You have seen many things, Face," She said. Her hand touched the silver of Her hair. She bit her lip. Her fingers shook a little when She touched the wrinkles under Her eyes.

Then Her hands went again to the swell of Her stomach, and Her eyes dropped away from Her reflection. She felt the Baby inside kick, and She thought of the beautiful brown Man who was now Her Son. She pictured the muscle of His upper arm move in its sheath of skin and the largeness of the teeth in His turning head as He had called to Her just days before to swim with Him in the stream. Juno Lucina sighed. His teeth had once been so tiny.

Then She straightened and opened the black box. From it She drew a crescent pendant and clasped its silver chain about Her neck. Her robes made a whispering noise as She rose and gathered up a black hooded cape that lay rumpled on the bed. Throwing it about Herself, Lucina made Her way to the front of Her cave and stepped out into the evening.

On the other side of the stream, She met Her Son. He smiled at Her and reached for Her hand. Together the Queen of Light and the Sun King crossed a desert, climbed a mountain, and came to the sea. There, its prow beached and wrapped in seaweed, waited a boat with fire-bright sails.

Juno Lucina stood at the edge of the sea facing Her Son, hands holding His. The wind blew the black hood from Her head.

"I love you, Mother," said the Sun King.

A sound of grief came from Lucina, and She pulled Him to Her. "Good-bye, wonderful Son."

Eyes glistening, She watched as the Sun King climbed into the boat with the blinding sails. Hair streaming silver light, toes clamping the sand, She waited as the tide flooded nearer and nearer to the boat's mooring. Finally the waters loosed the boat,

176

raised it, and began to rinse it toward the west. Son and Mother waved and waved until They could see each other no longer.

Never would She see this Man again. Memories filled Her. A long time went by. Then Lucina unhooked the silver chain from Her neck and reached high to hang the crescent pendant in the sky. All was dark, but the light from Her face and hands caught on the curve of the crescent, and it glowed where it hung.

Juno Lucina pulled the hood about Her head again. Then She turned east for the homeward journey. There She would wait in Her cave home for the birth of the next Sun King.

Demeter
(DEM-uh-ter)
and Persephone
(per-SEF-uh-nee)

(Greece)

Introduction

The Goddess Demeter was once the Mother of the Great Triangle of Life, the Mystery of the Universe, complete in all Her parts: Creator, Preserver, Destroyer. *Meter* means "Mother," and *De* is the word for delta, the triangle-shaped letter of the Greek alphabet. Her name was thus a visual pun: it suggested both the sacred Vulva and the Great Three-in-One Mother. The Goddess Persephone, who later came to be seen as Maiden, Daughter of Demeter, and simultaneously Queen of the Underworld, was once simply another way of talking about the Goddess Demeter in Her Virgin and Crone aspects.

Classical Greek storytellers, however, working with a masculinized pantheon of deities, regularly split the Great Mother into many personalities, each with Her own superhuman story. The Great One was thus shaved into the Mothers, Daughters, Sisters, Wives, Consorts, and Victims of the Gods, raising to new heights the level of instruction about the workings of the relatively recently established patriarchal system.

The story of Demeter Herself once recapitulated the mystery of the planted seed. Her journey from flower to fruit, from seed to burial, and death to rebirth was once told annually in some tremendously healing way. Ancient writings praise, but do not detail, this annual ritual, called the Eleusinian mysteries. In the mystery ritual, the Daughter of Demeter was like the seed in the fruit. As the fruit holds the seed, so every seed holds the fruited plant within Herself, and so on endlessly.

Patriarchal bias did more violence to the how-and-why tale of the seed and its seasons than just splitting the Goddess into Her Mother and Daughter aspects. In the story of the kidnap and rape of Persephone by the God of the Underworld, it not only masculinized the originally Feminine Deity of the Deep but also postulated that rape was the Maiden's introduction into Her own life-giving sexuality. Tragically, this story may well have reflected a growing reality in a culture newly given to exercising power over people, places, and things, rather than cultivating a reverence for the power alive in every being.

I preserved in my tale of Demeter and Persephone the expression of the Great Goddess as Mother and Daughter. From an Earth-centered point of view, however, wisdom and growth in this story are not predicated on the experience of victimization, but on the choice to plumb one's own depths. Grains, seeds, jewels, and rocks all symbolize these Goddesses for me. I long for the days when we mothers and aunts invoke Demeter and Persephone with flowers, bath, and song at the passages of our children—when they first menstruate, when they first leave home.

The Beginning of the Four Seasons

NCE UPON A
time, a long, long time ago, there were no seasons. There were
no changes in the weather or the plants. Animals played outside
all the time, because the only season that the Earth knew was
Spring. Always there were hopping birds, chirping flowers, and
fluffy clouds in a blue, blue sky.

That was the time when the Great Goddess Demeter and
Her Daughter Persephone roamed the meadows and the hills,
picking flowers, laughing, and swimming in rivers that took
them whoosh! down to the next curve. There They climbed
from the water, skins glistening in the sun, and ran back to
throw Themselves in again, rush down in the water perfect
around Them, and start all over again. They did everything
together, Demeter and Persephone: They ate and ate of pears,
apples, and oranges. They ate bananas, persimmons, pomegranates, and grapes. They made grass and flower salads with dew

for dressing and necklaces of berries and nuts. They braided strands of golden barley into Their hair.

Demeter loved to sit on a rock and watch Her Daughter's brown legs flash when She ran with deer and wolf. Then She would loop Her skirts and join, and the Earth would bustle with the sound of feet and bees.

Demeter was so glad to have this Girl. Persephone was Her friend and Her mirror, and sometimes Demeter hugged Her grown-up Baby for joy.

One day Persephone wandered away for a longer time than She ever had before. When She came home to Demeter, She was quiet, and Her eyes were looking far away. "Where have you been, My Baby?" asked Demeter, and She tipped Persephone's chin up a little.

Persephone moved Her head down. "Out, Mother," said Persephone.

"What's wrong, Little One?" asked Her Mother.

"Nothing," said Persephone. "And I'm not little."

Her Mother fanned Her hand through Persephone's curls. "Of course You're not, My Baby," She said. "Of course You're not. Now come eat."

So They ate and They laughed. But the next day, Persephone stayed away a long time again.

When She came back, Demeter took both Her hands. "Tell Me," She said. "Sit down and tell Me."

"I have to go," Persephone whispered.

"Speak up, Persephone," said Her Mother. "You have to what?"

"I have to go," said Persephone.

"You what?" said Her Mother.

"I have to go away from You."

"What are You saying? What can You mean? You can't go. Persephone, We have everything here. We have the world, the whole world. What do You mean? Why? Where would You go?"

"I have to go, Mother. Down. I have to go under the Earth. There are jewels there, Mommy. I have to go."

181

"Oh, my darling Child. You can't. You can't go. It isn't safe. Tell Me You won't go."

Persephone loosed Her hands from Her Mother's. "Let's eat, Mommy," She said.

The next day, Demeter stood looking and looking for Her Daughter. When She finally came, Demeter grabbed Her and held Her. "Don't go. Oh, don't go, Persephone." The two of Them rocked back and forth, holding each other in the sun.

Finally, Persephone pushed away. Tears were on both faces. "I have to go. I don't know when I'll be back, but I'll be back. Good-bye." She threw a cloak over Her shoulders. As She ran, it billowed out behind Her like a sail.

Demeter stood frozen for an instant. Then She let out a cry, "NO!" and leapt after Her Daughter. She drew just near enough to see a huge rock rumble aside, Persephone disappear, and the rock move again over the opening.

Demeter flung Herself at the rock. It did not move. She moaned and steadied Herself. Then She eased Herself down and held Her head in Her hands. For a long time Her shoulders shook silently. Night came. She stayed.

Neither did She move the next day. She sat still and spoke to no one. For a week She did not change her place. She did not eat. There were circles under Her eyes. A sore grew on Her mouth.

When She shifted Her posture the next week, it was only to pull Her robe more tightly about Her. For the wind, always before easy and warm, had grown strong and cold.

Demeter's hair knotted in the wind. The birds and animals who had not heard Her voice in so long went away. Demeter tipped Her head up to the sky. "I wish only for a blanket to cover me," She cried out. And something white began to fall from the sky. It swirled and turned. Silently it began to cover the ground.

Demeter slept through the night and part of the next day. When She awoke the sky was gray, and all around Her and on Her feet and arms was the white blanket called snow.

No leaves could be seen. The trees scratched at the sky. No food could be found.

And still Demeter did not move.

Days and weeks went by. They turned into months.

Then one day, the sun was warm enough to begin to melt the blanket of snow. Demeter licked Her dry lips. Then She shrugged. With a great effort, She pushed Herself to Her feet. As soon as She did so, something came out of the ground where She had been sitting so long. Why, it was a flower! A tiny white flower.

Then Demeter felt the ground beneath Her move. The rock on which She'd sat uprooted itself and uncovered a flight of stairs leading down into the Earth. Demeter made a sharp noise and braced Herself against the rock. She peered into the opening.

Up the stairway came a Girl—trudging a little, as if She were tired, but with Her face turned upward. She was holding to Her waist the hem of Her robe, as if there were something bumpy and heavy inside the skirt.

Demeter stood frozen. Then the sun glinted off the Girl's curls.

"Persephone!"

"Mommy!" sang out the Girl, and She leapt up the last steps and into Her Mother's arms.

When She did so, She let loose the front of Her robes, and a thousand emeralds, rubies and sapphires, amethysts and diamonds spilled out all over the ground. And at each place they touched, the snow melted and a host of flowers sprang up— until all the ground around those dancing Goddesses was green and sparkling and the birds and animals were kicking and swooping with joy.

Now every year, since that time, we have Spring only once a year. We also have Summer and Fall to honor the time Persephone is growing and getting ready to go to the center of the Earth. And we have Winter, to honor the time when Demeter's heart is breaking for missing Her Daughter.

Mayahuel (MY-uh-you-EL)
Endlessly Milking One
(Central America)

Introduction

Mother Goddess Mayahuel of the Mexican agave plant is called Woman with Four Hundred Breasts. The agave plant, known as the Tree of Life, is spiral shaped. Its central bulb is a kind of cave dripping with a milky elixir that is fermented to make pulque, the Mexican national beverage. It is drunk in order to nourish the crops, to celebrate the harvest, and to call for longevity in this world and the next. People use the milk of the Goddess Plant for birth ceremonies involving the umbilical cord and baptism.

Mayahuel, Mother Pot of the World, is imaged as a frog with a mouth in every joint of Her body; as the Lady on the turquoise throne; and as Mother to a suckling fish. Her story, connected to those of other cultures around the world, dates far beyond recorded Central American history. Her name and Her role as Goddess of pleasure, intoxication, and hallucination are both related to Maya of India, Goddess of the stuff of life's illusion (see story). She was called Maia by the Greeks, Maga by the Irish, and Maj by the Scandinavians. Like the archaic Greek Artemis, Mayahuel has many breasts and suckles a fish, the powerful symbol of transformation borrowed by the Christians for their own Fish Son, Jesus. Her consort, Ehecatl (eh-HEH-cah-tle), the Wind God, is related to both Quetzalcoatl and Tlaloc, whose images as the serpent and the rain suggest, not an opposition to Earth, but a blessed marriage of two forces, Earth and Sky, who need each other for the world to go on.

I regard the story of Mayahuel as a pre-Christian story of Mary and Christ, replete with the tremendously powerful archetypal themes of birth, separation, death, sacrifice, and rebirth. Indeed, in order to milk for myself an understanding of Mayahuel's story, I walked in a graveyard and told myself the Jesus story of my childhood. Reluctant at first to delve again into a saga in which Mary's part, for example, is so bridled and meek, I was arrested instead by the Bible story's characters, whose passion, tenderness, and courage lie just beneath the veil of modern patriarchal religious convention.

The figure of a frog and a red stoneware pot in the shape of a woman both remind me of Mayahuel's endless capacity for transformation and sustenance. The fish sign of the Christians has new meaning for me as Mayahuel's Fish Son.

The Story that Never Ends

O YOU WANT
to hear the story that never ends? Yes? Yes! Here is the story
that never ends.

Out of the four hundred bloody mouths of the Frog God-
dess Mayahuel came all the creatures of the world. And then
Mayahuel, Endlessly Bleeding One, took up Her jewel green
Frog skin and made of it a band for the sand-white garment Her
Woman form would wear. Into that dress She stepped, and into
Her nose She fastened a plate of blue. Into Her hair the color
of flames She bound the feathers of the eagle. Their soft points
sprang out about Her face like the rays of the Sun.

Then into the waters at Her feet She looked and showed
Her teeth with pleasure. She saw She was supple as a tongue
and lovely as a dewy night under the full of the Moon. She
called then, sweet and throaty, to Snake-the-Wind, singing and
crooning, holding Her breasts and whispering His name.

"Beautiful Ehecatl," sang the Goddess Mayahuel. "Blow to Me, bend to Me, My Treasure, My Wind."

Snake-the-Wind quickened when He heard the voice of His beloved. His nostrils opened and His lips parted. With lithe fingers, He clothed His Wind self in the skin of the Snake. His chest swelled. He bent and He blew.

"Ehecatl!" the voice of Mayahuel was thin with joy.

"Mayahuel, I come!" the voice of Snake-the-Wind was gigantic with hope. He slithered and surged. Mayahuel knelt and rocked. When Snake-the-Wind arrived, He slipped Himself between Her elbows and Her waist and wrapped Himself about Her swaying back. The eyes of Mayahuel and Snake-the-Wind sang to each other a thousand hymns. The tips of the tongues of Mayahuel and Her Wind Snake touched. Ehecatl bit the shoulder of His Goddess, and Mayahuel took His long and lovely length into Her arms.

Out of the union of Mayahuel and Ehecatl was born a Son in the shape of a Fish. To birth this Son, Mayahuel breathed and moaned, and Ehecatl rubbed sweet oil into Her belly and then caught the child that plunged gleaming from Her center. Mayahuel rested then against Ehecatl, who stroked Her hair.

Then, to suckle Her water Child, She grew four hundred Woman breasts where the four hundred mouths of Her Frog self had been. Now the Endlessly Bleeding One was the Endlessly Milking One, and the Fish Son's skin grew fat and orange with health.

Surely this Son had come to magnify life's abundance, for no matter the cares of His thousand questions or His busy interruptions to Their love, the Child brought to Mayahuel and Ehecatl a joy that deepened as He grew.

It came to pass that this well-beloved Son of the Endlessly Milking One and Snake-the-Wind took the form of a Boy. How the Mother and Father cherished this Child with His snapping eyes and soft mouth that told Them stories! For the Fish Boy Son had begun to travel, staying in the homes of the creatures of the world, listening to them and taking His impressions as a creature Himself. And so the innocence of His infanthood peeled away, leaving in its place a wisdom colored with energy and tinged with sadness.

One evening when the shadows were long, Mayahuel caught a look on the Fish Son's face that filled Her with a kind of dread. She saw that His was the face of a Boy no longer. His was the face of a Man now, at the same time restless and peaceful with purpose.

Mayahuel hovered at the edge of the dark. She felt swollen with feeling.

"It is the creatures," said Her Son, in answer to Her query. "I am come that they might have life, and have it more abundantly."

Mayahuel felt a thread of relief inside Her. "They have that in You, Son. They have that in You. You inspire them, Son. Their lives are richer, I know, for Your visits and Your stories."

Fish Son turned to look at His Mother, and His eyes were very kind. "I have the gift of stories, Mother," He said. "But inspiration is not enough when the creatures are hungry. I have also the gift of green, Mother. And I must give that, too."

Mayahuel felt Her throat tighten. The relief had fled. "How will You do that, My Son?" She whispered.

Fish Son reached out His hands to His Mother's. She took them in Her own. Both Their eyes were swimming with tears.

"I will take Fish form again, Mother. And I will lie out of the water and I will die. Then You will cut Me in pieces and bury Me. And then I will come to You and the creatures in a new form."

Mayahuel felt the mouths of Her Frog self loosen inside Her. She saw the dress of Her Woman self muddy and torn. She felt the shrivel of Her four hundred breasts, and She let Her Son take Her into His arms.

"It is good that You didn't argue with Him," said Snake-the-Wind. And the Mother and Father clung to each other until the morning came.

When Fish Son died, the Goddess Mayahuel made of Her four hundred breasts four hundred eyes. She cut up and buried Her beautiful Son and watered His grave with a river of tears.

From Fish Son's body deep in the wet Earth sprang up seed-bearing plants for the creatures of the world. From His hair came cotton; from His nostrils the herb for curing fevers. From His toes came the sweet potato, and out of His knees grew the maize. Indeed, to a thousand times four hundred, Fish Son's body made all of the fruits and grains of this world. The creatures of the world rejoiced and gave thanks over and over again for the gift of green.

Then the Goddess Mayahuel closed Her four hundred eyes and began to sing the song of the story that never ends. She sang it round and round and formed of Herself the maguey plant, a deep green cactus shrub with four hundred hard, pointed leaves in a rosette spiral. Into the plant She poured Herself; into its blossom She hummed the love of Herself and Her Ehecatl. "Neither drought nor hail nor cold touch Us here, My Beloved," She sang. And She filled Herself with the wine of Her endless milking.

Endlessly milking is Mayahuel to this very day. When under Her the creatures of the world put their pots, storing Her milk for the pulque of intoxication and blessing, they hear (yes they do!) in Her voluminous white essence the story that never ends.

Recovery of Herstory

Acquiring knowledge of personal history is life changing. It shifts attitude, action, and even circumstance; things are never the same again. Deep pieces fall into place when the secrets are revealed. Adopted child meets birth mother. The "big brother" is really the father and "mama" is really the grandmother. The meaning of the life-long nightmare is the childhood sexual abuse she never remembered until now. The "nervousness" is really mental illness; the "bad moods" are really alcoholism. The "terrible shame" is actually a first divorce or a baby "out of wedlock." Whether the news is good or bad, we are relieved. The gnawing feeling that the story as told just does not make sense falls away. The truth is out: we are whole.

Like secrets in an individual family, our collective herstories have been hidden from us. Not only have our "photos" been destroyed and "family" mythologies doctored, but the "documents" have been altered and even completely rewritten.

The commonly accepted Western history, for example, that humankind leapt from cave to the biblical era to Greece in a continuous stream of patriarchally dominated culture is a colloquial lie so pervasive that it is hard to ascribe ill will to it. After all, one historian simply starts where another leaves off, and no one, until Riane Eisler, Marija Gimbutas, Barbara Mor, Monica Sjöö, and Merlin Stone, has questioned the assumptions or "facts" of this story. On the contrary, like children who repress hunches and inconsistencies in family mythology, historians and their publics have swallowed facts that are not facts and interpretations that rob us of our ability to know who we are.

Patriarchal Western "history" renders invisible the stories of ancient Europe. Long explained as a land of barbarians until the Greeks rose up out of historical void, Europe was actually peopled with women and men who together created civilizations focused on art, trade, agriculture, and architecture. From the ruins and artifacts of their cities, we know these people neither expected nor perpetrated war; they valued the creative and worshiped the Goddess. As long ago as seven thousand years before what we accept as the common era, ancient European civilizations honored life in a way we are both shocked and thrilled to learn. We are shocked that we have not been told. How could they pretend that men have always dominated? Why did they not tell us that matrifocal civilizations fell at the hands of patriarchal invaders, who then borrowed their knowledge while degrading their lands and rewriting their records? The lies, we find, also blanket the "middle ages." Women were healers, then, burned by the millions as witches in order that male doctors borrow their knowledge, take their lands, and rewrite their records. The story of the burning times has been silenced; only in the code of fairy tales in which witches are alive, but demonic can we glimpse the power once held by women spiritually connected to Earth.

We are shocked, stung in a way that even all our cynicism and sophistication will never completely heal. But we are also thrilled. We are living in the times when the secrets are out. We are naming them, touching them alone and together. We are closing our eyes and letting our bones tell us what it must have been like. Suddenly all the dropped stitches are picked up again. We are finding Her image and presence in every country, every continent. We are telling Herstory: we are telling our stories. Our hearts, so afraid for the future, are madly borrowing hope from the past.

Lilith (LILL-ith)
Lady of the Air
(Middle East)

Introduction

R elated to the Sumerian Goddess Ninlil, Lady of the Air Who Gave Birth to the Moon, Lilith, Hand of Inanna (see story), is identified with the lily or lotus. The lily is the Great Mother's flower Yoni, which begets Herself and the world (see stories of Juno and Astarte). The sweeping sexuality of Her Person characterizes the endless mysteries of growing things over which She once unquestionably ruled. Her powers, however, were politically unacceptable to the nomadic tribes who coveted the fields of Her farming peoples. The nomadic story-tellers, therefore, invented a degrading biography for the Lady of the Moon.

Except inasmuch as Her image was collapsed into that of Lucifer, the Goddess Lilith lost Her place entirely in the Judeo-Christian Bible. In both Eve and the serpent, biblical writers subverted images of the Creator Goddess honored by earlier Middle Eastern creation myths. In Eve, they reduced the One

Who is Complete to wife of the first man, subordinate and obedient, experiencing sexuality for procreative purposes only. The snake, who possesses the secret of the Tree of Knowledge, is a disguised and diabolized version of the Goddess Herself. And Eve's very rebellion hints of the wisdom of the Great Feminine.

Rabbinical writers, on the other hand, retained the Divine Lady in the form of the Night Hag in the mystical book of the Kabbalah (see story of the Shekina). They wrote Lilith Herself into the script—as Adam's first wife. She refuses to do Adam's bidding, however, and flies away when he insists that She forego Her ancient position of pleasure and lie beneath him. While God creates Eve, Adam's second wife, in this story, Lilith takes the form of a She-Demon who spends Her evenings in the beds of dreaming men, milking them for nightly ejaculate and making of their sperm a hundred new demons a day. Beautiful temptress She is, they tell us, with long waving hair and claws for feet, like a bird of prey (see story of Cerridwen).

It is easy to see Eve and Lilith as two Sisters, both degraded versions of the Goddess who, split from each other, represent two halves of a once-sacred sexual whole. Eve is the Sister of Pregnancy and Motherhood; Lilith is the Sister of Menstruation and Independence. Integrated, They represent a body of wisdom that scorns the intellectualization of truth. Penelope Shuttle and Peter Redgrove have helped me to understand the connection of Eve and Lilith through their book, *The Wise Wound: Menstruation and Everywoman.*

I wrote Lilith's story as a kind of political cartoon, playing with the biblical creation myth's teaching that humans are to set themselves superior to the animals. Lilith, who can be represented by a juicy, saucy red apple, is the Goddess for me who lauds the kind of knowing that builds no hierarchy.

The First Woman and the Gift of the Moon

N THE BEGIN-
ning was the woman Lilith and the man Adam. They were wife
and husband and lived in a garden called Eden. The garden was
so green it rested the eyes like a cool cloth. Its fruits were as
many as the stars of the sky. Together Lilith and Adam grew
to know the plants and animals they lived with and to lie together, quiet and joyful, under the whispering trees.

But one day Adam took an idea into his head. "Lilith," said
Adam, "let's think up a name for each of the animals."

"I don't see a need for that, Adam. Seems like we're all just
fine here without names," said Lilith.

But Adam liked his new idea, and he began to spend whole
days picking just the right sound for each creature. All day he
paced and thought and named animals. Even at dinner he continued his project.

One day Adam said to Lilith, "Lilith, have you ever noticed how big I am? Why, I'm way bigger than you. See?" Adam showed his muscles. "And look how tall I am."

Lilith looked quietly at Adam.

"Lilith, you know what my name is going to be?" said Adam. "King. King. I'm king of this garden."

"I don't like the sound of that, Adam," said Lilith.

"It doesn't really matter if you like the sound, Lilith," said Adam. "I am the biggest and the strongest. So you've got to do what I say."

"You know, Adam, there are other ways to measure bigness than in inches, and other ways to measure strength than in muscles," said Lilith.

"Oh, come on, Lilith," said Adam. "I'm the king, and you're my queen."

"That's not for me, Adam," said Lilith. "The way I see it is that we're all sisters and brothers in this garden. Each of us is as important as the other. Nobody's king and nobody's queen."

Adam didn't listen, so Lilith walked away. The third time Adam started the argument, Lilith took herself out of the garden. Through its gates she went and into the Netherworld. There she sat still and quiet in the dark.

Adam was so furious at Lilith's leave-taking that even when he married the woman Eve and had a family of children, he continued to fume against her. "Snake lover!" he spat. "Not a woman, but a demon!"

"Hush, Adam!" said Eve. "Not in front of the children!"

Lilith alone in the Netherworld grew large. She was going to have a child. Waiting for the child, She gathered a gift to give to the sons and daughters of Adam and Eve. To a girl and a boy sleeping deep in a field She sent the dream of farming.

Soon after that dream was dreamed by the girl and the boy, Lilith had Her child. On a black night at the edge of the sea, hanging hard to the dark with Her hands and pushing against it with Her feet, Lilith gave birth to the Moon.

Astarte (uh-STAR-tay)
The Guiding Star
(Middle East)

Introduction

To the Semites of Canaan, Mesopotamia, and Arabia, lands we now call Lebanon, Israel, Syria, and Iraq, the Goddess Astarte was Queen of Heaven. Some of the earliest written material ever found details Her worship in periods that predate and coincide with biblical sagas. The judges and prophets of Old Testament stories repeatedly call for Her destruction. Their diatribes suggest that the Hebrews, often thought to be a homogeneous group, were actually a combination of roving tribes and settled cities, only some of whom were willing to adopt one Sky God over the Mother of All Baalim or Gods.

The judge Jeremiah, for example, records the Hebrew women's rage and sorrow against the suppression of worship of their Guiding Star. They take to the streets, shouting. Famine and want have followed Her cancellation, they chant. But Jeremiah, fist raised, admonishes them that the real cause of the current agricultural disaster is the people's refusal to worship Yahweh.

The story clearly suggests that natural calamity abetted the repression of the Goddess, both by physically weakening Her worshipers and by creating in them the psychology of despair that can so easily shift allegiance. The children of Israel had built shrines to the Queen of Heaven in city towers, on hills, in groves, and under every green tree. But Yahweh-worshiping Hebrews invaded their neighbors under orders from their Lord to "utterly destroy all the places . . . to break in pieces the images and cut down the groves, and fill [those] places with the bones of men" (Deuteronomy 12:2–3; 2 Kings 23:14). The Israelite queen Maacah was dethroned for worshiping the Lady in a grove (1 Kings 15:13).

Called Athtar, Attar, Attart, and Ishtar, Astarte is one of the oldest forms of the Goddess in the Mideast. The same creating, preserving, destroying Goddess worshiped by all Indo-European cultures, She was related to Hathor, Isis, Urania, Demeter, and Aphrodite. Mother of All Souls, Astarte ruled over the Spirits of the Dead who, with the light of Heaven for their robes, took the form of stars. Associated with the sea and the serpent, and ancient prototype of the Virgin Mary, Astarte's sacred drama in Syria and Egypt reenacted the rebirth of the solar God from this Celestial Virgin every December 25 (see story of Juno Lucina). Symbol of Her ability to regenerate Herself, the World, is Her lily, the same as the lily-lotus of Juno and Lilith (see stories). Northern Europeans called Her Ostara or Eostre, from which Her sacred "Easter lilies" are derived.

Astarte's Yoni or sacred Vulva was also represented by the Hebrew word *hor*—synonymous with hole, cave, or pit—representing both the Goddess Herself and Her priestesses, by whose sexual rituals the unclean could purify themselves. Diving into the pool of water in the sanctum of Her temple symbolized the sexual intercourse by which a man could realize "horasis" or spiritual enlightenment (very likely a precursor to the rite of baptism). Modern scholars, schooled to the concept that sexuality is at best simply a matter of physical fertility, have misnamed the hundreds of images of Astarte they have found buried by Her worshipers in the Earth. Calling them "fertility figures" misrepresents Astarte Quadesh, That Which is Holiness. Tireless Guide of Humankind, Lady of the Lands, the Goddess Astarte was none other than Sovereign of the World.

I wrote Astarte's story as an antidote to the painful series of Bible stories in which worshipers of "idols" are murdered and their cities, animals, and crops burned. I am moved by images of Astarte fashioned of clay by circles of women and quick-baked in the kitchen oven while we sing, talk, and eat together in the living room.

The Burning of the Lady's People

AMA, WHY ARE the stars cold?" Sal asked his mother one afternoon as she ground meal for bread. Sal had carried a pot of water from the well at the city square, and now he sat down in the shade of the porch near his mother and baby sister who slept in a basket nearby.

"I don't think they *are* cold, little lamb," said his mother. "I think they just seem cold because they're so far away. But you know what they really are?"

"What?" said Sal.

"They're all the children of the Guiding Star, our Astarte," said Sal's mother.

"The stars are Her babies?" asked Sal.

"Yes," said his mother. "They're all the spirits of the people ever in the world—before they are born and after they die."

"Is Grandma a star then?" asked Sal.

"Yes, and you were a star before you came to live with me and Daddy."

"Was Sister too?" said Sal.

"Yes," said his mother.

Sal was quiet. Then he said, "Mama."

His mother looked up. She stopped grinding meal. "What, Sal?" she asked.

"Mama, if Daddy gets killed will he turn into a star?"

"Yes, sweetheart," said his mother, and she opened her arms. Sal went to stand inside her hug, and he felt her warmth. "But, Sal, I think Daddy's going to come home safe for us," she whispered.

Sal lived thousands of years ago in a big city in a land called Canaan. Sal's family and all the other families in that city worshiped the Great Mother Astarte. Astarte's big temple sat at the center of the city, and every home held a little altar for Astarte right next to the oven where they baked their bread. Each family kept beautiful things on its altar: lovely cloth and delicious fruits and a small clay figure of Astarte in the shape of a Mother with a baby inside Her. Sal's daddy said that was to remind the people that Astarte was always making new life. Sal's mother said Astarte never slept and She helped life grow and She also made dying. It was like a big circle, his mother said. Being born, growing, getting old, and dying and then back to being born again.

This was a frightening time for the people in Sal's city. Sal's daddy and a lot of other boys and men had marched out of the city in an army. When Sal asked his father why, his daddy said it was because the invaders were coming.

"What's invaders?" asked Sal.

"They're people who want our land," said Sal's father.

"Why?" said Sal.

"I don't know," said his father. "But Daddy's going to make sure you and Mama and Sister are safe."

"When will you come back, Daddy?" asked Sal.

"As soon as I can," said his father.

It seemed to Sal that his daddy was gone a very long time. Then one day, Sal and his friends were playing sticks at the gate to the city. Suddenly, a boy said, "Hey! Look!" When the others looked, they could see a cloud of dust in the distance.

"It's Daddy!" said Sal. "Maybe the army's back!"

The children didn't play anymore. They just watched the cloud of dust puff bigger and bigger. When they could see people in the distance, they began to run toward them.

The men waved when they saw the children, but there were so many of them that the children, instead of trying to find their own brothers and fathers and uncles, raced back to the gates of the city. Shouting the news, they ran through the streets.

"They're home!" yelled Sal. "Mama, Mama, Daddy's coming!"

Sal's mother got tears in her eyes. She hugged Sal hard. Sal's little sister clapped her hands and crowed.

"Mama, Mama, come on! He's almost here!" Sal pulled on his mother's arm.

Sal's mother kissed Sal's head. "Lamb, he won't come here right away," she said.

"Mama, why? He's home," said Sal.

"I know, Sal, but first he must go to the temple."

"Why?" asked Sal.

"Well, for Daddy to come back and eat with us and love us and live with us, he has to get the war and fighting off him," said his mother.

"How, Mama?" asked Sal.

"Well, Astarte's priestesses will take away his war clothes and bathe him and feed him holy food and hug him and sing to him. Then they will give him home clothes and he can come back to us," said his mother.

Sal's little sister crawled across the floor and a neighbor burst into the room. "They're home, Rebia!" she said to Sal's mother. "Did you see your daddy, Sal?" she asked.

Sal stopped. "No, but he's coming," Sal said.

"Sal!" said his mother. Her voice sounded high and anxious.

"I thought you said you saw him!"

"I saw *them*, Mama," said Sal. "I know he's coming."

Well, Sal was right. The days it took seemed very long, but Sal's daddy did return home. He gathered Sal and his mother and little sister into his arms and held them all very close. "How I've missed you!" he said, and wiped away his tears.

"Daddy!" said Sal. "Did you kill the invaders?"

"No, Son," said his father. "There are many, many invaders, and they move in small groups, so they are hard to find."

Sal's little sister gurgled, and Sal climbed on his daddy's lap.

"Rebia," said Sal's father to his mother. "The invaders are burning whole cities."

Sal's mother picked up her little girl. Sal could see that his mother's eyes were frightened.

"People say that the invaders have a god that wants all the land."

"And the people on the land?" whispered Sal's mother.

"It's bad, Rebia," said Sal's daddy.

Sal looked at his parents' faces, trying to understand. "Daddy, why?" said Sal. "Why can't they share the land? Why can't we all live here?"

"Sal, that's a very good question. And I don't know the answer," said his father. "Rebia, I want us to bury our Astarte."

Sal's little sister began to cry. Sal's mother's lips turned very pale. "What are you thinking?" she asked.

"Rebia, I'm thinking that no matter what happens, I want to save the idea of our Great Mother," said Sal's father.

That night Sal's family stayed very close together. After they ate, Sal's mother and father dug a hole next to the oven. Sal got to put the little figure of the Mother with the baby inside Her into the ground and help press dirt on top of Her. Sal's mother many times chanted the name *Astarte* and some other words Sal couldn't understand.

"Daddy?" asked Sal. "Why doesn't Astarte want all the land, like the invaders' god?"

"Sal, Astarte *is* the land," said Sal's father. "She is all the animals and all the plants and all the waters and all the sky. She is the soil and the wind."

"And the stars too?" asked Sal.

"The stars too," said his father.

The invaders did not come right away. But they did come. And they burned the city Sal lived in and all its people.

Why? you might ask.

It's very hard to understand, and we don't really know the answer to that question. But Sal's father had a very good idea when he buried the figure of Astarte. There have been many invaders and many wars since that time so long ago. Many people have lived and died, and many people have hurt the Earth because they did not know about Astarte.

But not so long ago, people began to find little figures of Astarte deep in the ground in the place where Sal's city stood so long ago. "Who could this be?" they asked themselves. And slowly they pieced together the story of the Great Star Mother. "She's still here," they say to each other. "She's still here after all this time."

Lamia (LA-mee-uh)
Snake Woman
(North Africa)

Introduction

L amia is ancient as the Snake Herself in the desert-oasis land of Libya, once the name of all of northern Africa except for Egypt. Most probably She was worshiped by Libyan-Berber peoples, a light-skinned, nomadic group of Africans whose descendants still herd camels, goats, and sheep in the Sahara and the mountainous areas of Algeria, Morocco, and Tunisia. Associated historically with the ancient Goddess-worshiping Amazons of Herodotus's history, the Berbers today are connected with North Africa's Tuareg people. The position of the Tuareg woman is unique in the Islamic world. Veilless, she is able to demand monogamy and divorce. She marries relatively late, and enjoys an unguarded sexual life prior to marriage. Guardian of tradition, she writes tribal script, keeps alive legend, myth, and song, and is expert user of herbal cures. Succession is through her line, rather than her husband's.

The ancient Greeks were greatly influenced by the Libyans. They borrowed Lamia for stories of their own making, stories that not so much stripped the Goddess of Her power, but eroded the people's relationship with Her so that it no longer challenged them to probe Her endlessly renewing mystery. Medusa is the Greek name for Lamia; the Serpent Goddess is known too as Neith, Athene, Anatha, Buto, and, in ancient Babylonia, Lamashtu. Called Mother of Gods, Daughter of Heaven, and Great Lady, Her name was used in the European Middle Ages as a general term for witch or demon in the shape of woman.

I collect and write the stories in this book in the context of a patriarchy under increasing pressure to change. The stories are also branded with my reaction to my fundamentalist Christian background and my intense interest in feminism, spirituality, and mythology itself. Historically, tellers of the story of the Snake Goddess Lamia were similarly affected by cultural pressures, personal histories, and particular audiences. The story of Lamia in this collection is my version of how their versions perhaps developed.

All powerful archetypes undergo tremendous change as current cultural forces shape them. We may glimpse the power the Goddess once held just by observing the breadth and depth of changes wrought on Her mythologies. Changes in the story of the Snake Woman Goddess are particularly exemplary. The snake, once unquestionably revered, underwent a stunning reversal of status. From reverence to revulsion, from mystery to mockery She fell. Only forces of disrespect, misuse, and cruelty could have been at work in the lives of people who began to view the snake's transforming power as evil rather than awesome.

Pictures and readings about the snake can invoke Lamia. This Goddess in my life is the agony and beauty of changing slowly and absolutely.

How the People of Today Have Two Stories

VER SINCE THE beginning, fear of Lamia, the Snake Woman, has coiled in the bellies of all who sense Her majesty and mystery. She may be tensed and swaying, upright in readiness. She may unhinge Her jaws and swallow a fat and complex life into Her own thin, simple length. We watch Her, and our fingernails dig into the soft flesh of our palms. And when She lies white as death, with eyes blind and darting tongue still, our own eyes turn deep into the unanswered, and we are afraid. We look in wonder when She climbs without arms or legs from Her dull and brittle coat into the new one soft and vividly colored. We are relieved. She is alive. We are full of hope. She returns again. But we feel afraid. Yes, with Lamia, Snake Woman of the deepest dance we know, we are a little afraid. It has always been so!

It was so at the beginning of the First People. They were the people of the limitless dunes at the edge of the stunning blue sea, the people of the cliffs bordering the dry rivers. They were the people who observed and copied their Snake Woman to receive the gift of the oasis.

There in the land where the wind blows in yellow pillars and the heat is cruel, the First People in the desolate morning formed a great circle with Snake Woman at their center. They held hands and danced to the drums that copied the slow beat of Lamia's heart. The First People's dance was measured and even, and Snake Woman, head and neck hidden by a cloth, sang and swayed at the center. "Who are you, Lamia?" the First People called to Her, wondering and afraid, pitching their voices low, sedate, and simple like the body of the Snake at the center.

"Copy Me and you shall see," answered Lamia over and over again.

The First People paced out Her rhythm again and again, smoldering, undulating, bodies and voices turning in exhausted circles, slinking toward the afternoon.

"Who are we, Lamia?" the people sang.

"Copy Me and you shall see," answered Snake Woman.

The people trickled out their sound and their sweat. Their feet and their hair turned hot and limp. And when the sun stood finally at the bottom of the sky, the desert blossomed. The dunes were dahlia red, the sand floor mustard yellow. The hills turned coral and violet, and the stepping people spoke by turns.

"She is the Deep and the Wet One."

"She is the Necklace of Life under the sand."

"We are the jewel keepers."

"We are the builders of the vats."

When the dark came, then, the sky blazed with stars, the drums grew silent, and Lamia's people dreamed of plumbing the underground water for the figs, palms, oranges, pomegranates, and almonds of the oasis.

Lamia's First People drew from the basin of Her rocks Her water gift. From those precious wells came the moisture to grow the barley, the wheat, the millet, the onions, and the tomatoes beside the skeletons of riverbeds and streams. The size of the oasis grew by threes, and in gratitude and wisdom Her First People continued to copy Her rhythm.

The First People of Lamia copied Her deadness. They unhinged their jaws to mimic Her swallowing of life. They lay without moving or moaning. "You are like the ghibli winds," they sang to Her. "You leave nothing living, not even the fetus in the mother's womb."

The People copied Lamia new and large and young again. "You are like the winds of the north," they crooned. "Your waters draw shrubs from the Earth for our sheep to feed on. You make us fertile, You make us virile, You fill our children with strength."

"It has always been so," went the hymn. "It has always been so!"

One day it happened that a ship blew from the north over the sea. The ship, bound for trading with the People of Lamia, carried on it a sailor who entertained his brothers with stories he wove from the boredom and novelty of his adventures. The teller's quick words sometimes reminded his listeners of a child who works to comfort himself in the midst of fear.

Orestes, the teller, was a small man with a scurrying gait. His hands busied themselves with carving or smoking or mending, and he asked his listeners often, "Do you know what I mean?" They answered as often that they did; their assurances encouraged him to continue and told this nervous, sweet-eyed man that all was well a little while longer.

The words of Orestes were fantastic, enchanting, and tragic. His tales could drive away hunger, shorten the night, and take the pain out of a lashing. Orestes said that's just why he told stories. Stories and mead, he said, could both numb the agony. He told of slaves yoked neck to neck, herded bare of foot over sharp rocks, the dead and ill cut away at night and left to make mountains of skulls at the crossings of the roads. Paradise, said Orestes, was a cave dripped over by a veil of tears. Like crystals, you could look through them and reach endlessly for what could have been but never will be. Orestes told of the caves of the Pythoness, the oracle at Delphi, who sees the future of kings in a cup of blood poured out of the moon and keeps Her children in soft-shelled eggs under Her heart. He told of ships that could fly and nectars shared by truced armies at banquets before the slaughters of betrayal began.

And privately, to his sad-eyed companion, the farmer boy with the tremulous, constant smile, the teller spoke of his mother, slave of the inner house, who nestled him sometimes and beat him at others, and whose food turned to poison if he tried to eat too much of it. Sometimes there were whippings that left him for dead, "but all you can do," said Orestes, "is survive. Do you know what I mean?" The boy would smile and lean down against the outstretched leg of his friend and hold Orestes's ankle for a while in his rough young hand.

The day the ship docked on the northern coast of Africa, Orestes gave his two gold coins to his blond companion for safekeeping. "You keep these so's I won't drink too much," he said. The boy concealed them with a flicker of understanding in his pale eyes, and the two sailors went ashore to the traders' settlement at the edge of the land of the People of Lamia.

The keeper of the inn there was a muscular man with blue veins twining his forearms when he lifted pots of stew in his kitchen. He liked the stories of Orestes and so let him sweep and wash the cooking pots in exchange for his supper and a jug of mead. Orestes appreciated more than the food. He admired the innkeeper, and he borrowed the big man's tireless strength for the hero of new stories that he spun by the side of the fire for the evenings' boisterous customers.

Orestes, however, didn't take his bed at the inn. The air was too close there, he said. So he carried his jug and his blanket and slept with his companion under the dome of the sky. For the sky here in this strange land was king; and in its giant starry blackness pulsed a peace that thickened and melted around the two sailors as they drank and finally slept.

On a blinding blue day that followed a night of stories and mead, Orestes and his friend discovered the oasis. Throbbing from the night's liquor, the man and boy walked in the searing

212

heat until they came upon that place of green and water. Here, in this infernal land was shade and rest. And possibly more mead, thought Orestes, to mend this morning's sickness.

But the sailors found themselves calmed and frightened at the same time. For the People of Lamia had begun Her dance. Women and men alternating, holding hands in a circle. Slowly moving about the Snake at the center.

The sailors stared. Head and neck covered by a cloth, this center Snake raised Herself upright, coiling and swaying. With these people weaving steady and certain around Her, the Snake was still again. The sky pounded with the drum from the heart of the circle. In and out the people moved, close now, back, close again, sweat in curls down their faces and sides. Slowly, out and in, facing this Snake, pacing a pattern on the sand, the circle slithered and twisted, and the feet measured their rhythm into a sound that grew steady and smooth as the rain on a rock.

Orestes felt his head reel. The Snake at the center became like Woman to him, alive now and beautiful, then dead and unreachable. The dancers were the snakes now, twisting and ancient, lethargic as water, turning endlessly around this lunging, quiet beauty at the center Who held not just men, but women also, to Her bottomless flow of movement. Orestes and the boy could not understand the language of the People of Lamia. They could not know that Her People gained Her strength by imitating Her, that they knew Her answers by taking Her shape. Orestes and the boy understood little of this slowness; their own people's dances were speedy and wild.

Something terrified stirred in Orestes, and he began to shake. In the midst of the heat, his teeth chattered. The boy looked at the dancers and at the face of his friend. It was crumpled as a child's, and the boy, not smiling now, led Orestes by one chilled hand away from the oasis and back across the land to the sea. The boy made a fire and wrapped Orestes in two blankets. Then he held the man's hands.

"What happened?" asked the boy. Orestes didn't know. He could only say how strange it was, women dancing with men that way, and the Snake so pulsing at the center. "It was like

213

a dream, do you know what I mean?" said Orestes. "Like a dream."

The boy said yes, that seeing the snake made him think of the job he'd had lambing, where the newborns slipped into his hands, still connected to the ewes with cords like bloody snakes. He'd cut a cord when the throbbing stopped if the mama couldn't bite through it herself. "You feel scared when you do it," the boy said. "But it makes you feel good afterward. Seeing the lambs walking around, knowing they wouldn't if you hadn't helped." The boy stretched his lips again in his lonely, trembling smile and held Orestes while the older man drank from the jug of mead.

Because the Snake Woman stayed in the mind of Orestes, the storyteller, it so happened that Lamia, the Wet One of the Deep, became part of the stories of the land across the sea. But Orestes, the storyteller, knew neither Her dance nor the power of copying Her motions of life and death. Instead, he knew only the terrible cold that had swept him when he watched, ill from the night and unable to talk with Her people. He saw Her power and was afraid, and so he made in his own language a story of a Snake Woman who terrorized and could be subdued only by the bravest of men.

And so it is to this day. We are the people with both stories. Like the slender shape of Lamia Herself, our fear has followed the ripples of time, and we ask ourselves, as we have from the beginning, what to do with it. When we were the First People of Lamia, we watched Her and we copied Her. We learned and we were comforted. But when we are the people of Orestes, our oasis is only in our minds: there we crawl for comfort against the trampling and the slavery. We are afraid of this Lamia. Of Her imitation we know nothing. We try to control Her instead.

In our fear there is power; in Her power there is fear. Shall we copy Her? Can we control Her? We thirst and circle the winds in the deserts of our souls, wondering and dancing our decisions.

214

Yemaya (yeh-my-YAH)
and
Iamanja (hee-ah-mansh-YAH)
She Who Continues
(Yoruba People and Brazil)

Introduction

O ften depicted as a mermaid, Fish Mother Yemaya, Goddess of the Ogun River and the Sea, was worshiped by
the Yoruba people of Nigeria who were enslaved by traders and
carried in the stinking death holds of ships to the Americas.
Sent by the thousands mainly from the cities of Ife and Benin—
which had stood for four to five hundred years before the arrival
of the Europeans in 1500—the Yoruba people unwillingly settled British, French, Spanish, and Portuguese holdings in the
"new world." There they kept alive their pride and their Goddess to the present day in Brazil, Cuba, Haiti, and Trinidad.

In Brazil, Yemaya is called Iamanja. She is a powerful Sea
Mother, a Virgin Mary–like deity in the joyous Afro-Indo-
Catholic religion in which rapturous, ecstatic dance and song
summon Her might, power, and mana.

Brazilian slaves and free blacks maintained ties with Africa
almost entirely absent in the United States. For economic rea-

215

sons, slave trade ended in the northern hemisphere by 1808. Subsequently, most North American slaves were born in the United States, and memories of Africa grew dim. Slavery in Brazil, however, was not phased out until 1888, and crossings of blacks to Africa and back were frequent until 1905. *Malembos,* or friendships of solidarity and resistance among fellow captives, were nurtured by newcomers who spoke African languages and brought life-giving myths and stories of home. *Malembos* enabled the rise of *quilombos* and *mocambos* (forest hideouts), found all over Brazil from the sixteenth century on. On the *quilombos,* fugitives could protest the system that bound them; return to a life free of a master's role; and practice African religions in freedom. Other slaves organized open resistance in the spirit of *malembo* or found ways to buy their freedom. Former Brazilian slaves often returned to Africa, sometimes to become important figures in society there.

Urban, rather than rural-dwelling, blacks in Brazil were most able to maintain African rites and customs since they had the greatest freedom of movement and the strongest likelihood of meeting newly arrived slaves from their own nation who spoke their own language. To this day, Brazilians of many colors offer gifts of candles, food, perfume, flowers, and champagne to their Great Sea Mother. On New Year's Eve, they wash away the impurities of the old year in the waters of Iamanja. On December 8, they honor Her limitless mercy and protection. On the Summer Solstice, they float boats full of offerings on Her waves. Bathers count seven swells in Her name, reminiscent of the seven petticoats She is said to wear, before entering the sea. Fishermen call on Her for protection for their precarious, raftlike vessels. Iamanja's color is blue.

Unlike the radical tampering endured by the Libyan Goddess Lamia when Her story survived the crossing to Greece, the Nigerian Water Goddess Yemaya underwent changes that preserved Her glory and comfort for the people who call Her Iamanja in Brazil. Lamia's story was undoubtedly carried back to Greece by outsiders visiting Africa. Yemaya, on the other hand, became Iamanja when Her people, victims of the slave trade

organized by the culture of control, brought Her story themselves to the new continent. Tellers who thought they could
gain from the patriarchy changed Lamia from wondrous to hor-
rendous. Iamanja's tellers had everything to gain by psycholog-
ically defending themselves against a way of life that had broken
their connections with the land they called home.

I wrote the story of Yemaya and Iamanja to honor the or-
ganic process of change that stories undergo when their peoples
change. It is also the story of people who mend the rents in the
fabric of their lives with threads of rage, courage, love, and joy.

The Journey to the New Land

HEN WE WERE
the people of the round houses in the forests and the savanna,
when our mornings were peopled with spirits, You, River Woman,
Yemaya, were the flow that beat in our legs and hearts.

When time untwirled under Sky Keeper and clouds sang
over the heat of Your waters, You, Yemaya, floated and continued.

When Iron Maker cut the trees and we were the people in
the square house kingdoms at the edge of the land, You, River
Woman, widened Your skirts and continued into the sea.

When we were the people who knelt to Allah in the after-
noons, when we were the people who forgot Your name, You,
Yemaya, Sea Woman, continued.

When the bleached skins came and the stealing and selling
of people began, when the screaming and whipped of the round
houses were kicked to the coast to be branded and raped; when

square-house people took money for the round-housers, when the wail tore from our guts, You, River to Sea, surged and continued.

When we were the people in chains, huddled against the nursing among us who soothed us, wounds and mouths, with milk, when we were the strangled and the starving and stood sobbing, You, Sea Woman, salted our tears and continued.

When the bleached skins jerked us to the prison boats and we, the people, took the journey of putrefaction, when we prayed to die, when we danced off the decks into Your arms, You, Yemaya, Endlessly Swelling One, cold, clean, deep sleep, You continued.

When we were the people at the markets of the new coast, when the bleached skins had clothes and we could cover only our genitals, when we were taken sister from brother, mother from child, father from kin, when our livers were broken inside us, You, Lady of the Sea, Star of the River, You, Yemaya, continued to pulse.

When in the light and the air once again we could feel Your sureness, when we wove a language of homes in this new place, when we called You Iamanja and dressed You in seven waves for petticoats, You, Star of the Sea, Lady of the River, drummed in our shoulders and feet.

When we were the people in the cities of the new land, when we moaned for the trees and curves of home, when we knew rage and sorrow like knives and bile in our throats, You called us to You, Iamanja, and continued.

When we were the ones who wanted to die, Your waters carried to us new arrivals from our homes, new ones for us to care for and comfort, new ones with old stories of You in words that were lullabies in our ears and sweet home fruits in our mouths. When we would curse You and forget You, You continued, Lady of Compassion, You continued.

When the new ones' fury filled our spines with hope, when we planned and ran, when we made *quilombos* away from the masters, safe in the balmy woods, when we drank of You free and in peace far from the coasts of the new land, You blessed us, Lady of Purification, You continued.

When we braided You, Iamanja, Star of the Sea, with the Lady Maria of the Cross and the Spirits of the brown skins deep in the forests, when we knew You newer, wider, feasting, bathing, nesting us with the tender pride of the grandmothers we could never know, when You continued to undulate, Water Woman, our souls found a way to be quiet and dance.

When the rapes and the loves, Iamanja, made skins no more just black and brown and bleached, but all the shades between, when we were the people who bought our own freedom and the people who returned to the home of the beloved trees and curves, when the square-house people of Allah listened to our slave stories with shame and respect, when we became leaders in the old land, You, Protectress of Journeyers, You continued.

When we were the people the law loosed from bondage, You surged, Lady Maria, You continued.

When we were the people in the new land folding like meat into broth magic, desire, and passion into the worship of Maria, when we taught You could not enter us if we did not dance, when we said the bravest ones in the world are those who love, You, Iamanja, Mighty Woman of the Ebb, of the blind swaying plants, of the seven sacred petticoats, You continued.

When we are the sisters and brothers of the many skins who gather in a house, when we, coming together, break the shackles of the city and hoist You up to ride us, horses galloping through Your waves, ride us, arms clinging, to meet ourselves, when we are the sweaters of ecstasy, the fish people of the deep, You, Queen of the River, Empress of the Sea, You of the Flowers, the Perfume, Precious One, You continue to continue.

Book List

Adler, Margot. *Drawing Down the Moon*. Boston: Beacon Press, 1987.

Airola, Paavo. *How to Get Well*. Phoenix, AZ: Health Plus Publishers, 1974.

Al-Anon's One Day at a Time. New York: Al-Anon Family Group Headquarters, Inc., 1978.

Al-Anon's 12 Steps and 12 Traditions. New York: Al-Anon Family Group Headquarters, Inc., 1984.

Bastide, Roger. *The African Religions of Brazil: Toward a Sociology of the Interpenetration of Civilizations*. Baltimore: Johns Hopkins Univ. Press, 1978.

Bernal, Martin. *Black Athena: The Afroasiatic Roots of Classical Civilization*. New Brunswick: Rutgers University Press, 1987.

Billington, James H. *The Icon and the Axe: An Interpretive History of Russian Culture*. New York: Random House, 1970.

Bowles, Paul. *Their Heads Are Green and Their Hands Are Blue: Scenes from the Non-Christian World*. New York: Ecco Press, 1963.

Bradshaw, John. *Healing the Shame that Binds You*. Deerfield Beach, FL: Health Communications, Inc., 1988.

Bolen, Jean Shinoda. *Goddesses in Everywoman*. San Francisco: Harper & Row, 1984.

————. *Gods in Everyman*. San Francisco: Harper & Row, 1989.

Budapest, Z. *Grandmother of Time*. San Francisco: Harper & Row, 1989.

Chatwin, Bruce. *The Songlines*. New York: Penguin Books, 1987.

Crocco, John A. *Gray's Anatomy*. New York: Bounty Books, 1977.

Degler, Carl N. *Neither Black nor White: Slavery and Race Relations in Brazil and the United States*. New York: Macmillan, 1971.

Downing, Christine. *Journey Through Menopause*. New York: Continuum, 1989.

Duerk, Judith. *A Circle of Stones*. San Diego: LuraMedia, 1989.

Dworkin, Andrea. *Woman Hating*. New York: E. P. Dutton, 1976.

Farrar, Janet, and Stewart Farrar. *A Witches Bible Compleat*. New York: Magickal Childe, 1987.

_____. *The Witches' Goddess*. Seattle: Phoenix, 1987.

Freuchen, Peter. *Book of the Eskimos*. Cleveland: World Publishing Company, 1961.

Gadon, Elinor. *The Once and Future Goddess*. San Francisco: Harper & Row, 1989.

Gendler, Ruth. *The Book of Qualities*. Berkeley: Turquoise Mountain, 1984.

Gerster, George. *Sahara: Desert of Destiny*. New York: Coward-McCann, Inc., 1960.

Gimbutas, Marija. *The Language of the Goddess*. San Francisco: Harper & Row, 1989.

Hall, Nor. *The Moon and the Virgin*. New York: Harper & Row, 1981.

Hay, Louise. *You Can Heal Your Life*. Santa Monica, CA: Hay House, 1987.

Johnson, Buffie. *Lady of the Beasts: Ancient Images of the Goddess and Her Sacred Animals*. San Francisco: Harper & Row, 1988.

Keith, Agnes Newton. *Children of Allah: Between the Sea and the Sahara*. Boston: Little, Brown, 1965.

MacKenzie, Donald A. *Myths of Pre-Columbian America*. Boston: Longwood Press, 1978.

Mattoso, Katia M. de Queirós. *To Be a Slave in Brazil*. New Brunswick: Rutgers Univ. Press, 1979.

Meldgaard, Jorgen. *Eskimo Sculpture*. New York: Clarkson N. Potter, 1960.

Mellody, Pia. *Facing Codependence*. San Francisco: Harper & Row, 1989.

Miller, Alice. *The Drama of the Gifted Child*. New York: Basic, 1983.

_____. *For Your Own Good*. New York: Farrar, Straus, 1983.

_____. *Thou Shalt Not Be Aware*. New York: New American Library, 1986.

Morrison, Boone; Malcolm Naea Chun. *Images of the Hula*. Volcano, HI: Summit Press, 1983.

Mukerjee, Radhakamal. *The Culture and Art of India*. New York: Praeger, 1959.

Pagels, Elaine. *The Gnostic Gospels*. New York: Random House, 1979.

Roberts, Jane. *The Nature of Personal Reality*. Englewood Cliffs, NJ: Prentice-Hall, 1974.

Schaef, Anne Wilson. *Co-Dependence: Misunderstood and Mistreated*. San Francisco: Harper & Row, 1985.

_____. *When Society Becomes an Addict*. San Francisco: Harper & Row, 1987.

_____. *Women's Reality*. San Francisco: Harper & Row, 1982.

Schafer, Edward H. *The Divine Woman: Dragon Ladies and Rain Maidens*. San Francisco: North Point Press, 1980.

Shuttle, Penelope, and Peter Redgrove. *The Wise Wound: Menstruation and Everywoman*. New York: Grove Press, 1988.

Sjöö, Monica, and Barbara Mor. *The Great Cosmic Mother: Rediscovering the Religion of the Earth*. San Francisco: Harper & Row, 1987.

Spretnak, Charlene. *The Spiritual Dimension of Green Politics*. Santa Fe: Bear & Co., 1986.

Stein, Gertrude. *The World is Round*. Berkeley: North Point Press, 1988.

Starhawk. *Dreaming the Dark*. Boston: Beacon Press, 1989.

_____. *The Spiral Dance*. San Francisco: Harper & Row, 1989.

_____. *Truth or Dare*. San Francisco: Harper & Row, 1987.

Stone, Merlin. *Ancient Mirrors of Womanhood*. Boston: Beacon Press, [1979] 1984.

_____. *When God Was a Woman*. New York: Dial Press, 1976.

Sturluson, Snorri. *Prose Edda*. Trans. by Jean I. Young Cambridge: Bowes and Bowes, 1954.

Swimme, Brian. *The Universe Is a Green Dragon*. Santa Fe: Bear & Co., 1984.

Teish, Luisah. *Jambalaya*. San Francisco: Harper & Row, 1985.

von Franz, Marie-Louise. *Problems of the Feminine in Fairytales*. Dallas: Spring Publications, 1972.

_____. *Shadow and Evil in Fairytales*. Dallas: Spring Publications, 1974.

Walker, Alice. *The Temple of My Familiar*. New York: Harcourt, Brace, Jovanovich, 1989.

Walker, Barbara. *The Crone*. San Francisco: Harper & Row, 1985.

_____. *The Skeptical Feminist*. San Francisco: Harper & Row, 1987.

_____. *The Woman's Encyclopedia of Myths and Secrets*. San Francisco: Harper & Row, 1983.

Weigle, Marta. *Spiders and Spinsters: Women & Mythology*. Albuquerque: Univ. of New Mexico Press, 1982.

Yarmolinsky, Avrahm, ed. *Two Centuries of Russian Verse: An Anthology*. New York: Random House, 1966.

Zimmer, Heinrich. *Myths and Symbols in Indian Art and Culture*. Princeton: Princeton Univ. Press, 1946.